TORT LAW SIMULATIONS

Jamie R. Abrams

University of Louisville Brandeis School of Law

BRIDGE TO PRACTICE SERIES®

WEST
ACADEMIC
PUBLISHING

Bridge to Practice Series® is a trademark registered in the U.S. Patent and Trademark Office.

© 2020 LEG, Inc. d/b/a West Academic
    444 Cedar Street, Suite 700
    St. Paul, MN 55101
    1-877-888-1330

West, West Academic Publishing, and West Academic are trademarks of West Publishing Corporation, used under license.

Printed in the United States of America

ISBN: 978-1-68467-314-8

ACKNOWLEDGMENTS

The author extends her warmest gratitude to the talented research assistants at the University of Louisville Brandeis School of Law who helped develop and edit these materials: Katie Davidson, Melissa Kapsalis, Kylie King, Erin Langley, Margaret Lawrence, Cat McCloskey, and Julie Tackett. The author also extends her heartfelt thanks to colleagues Valerie Weber and Marija Sasek of the University of Louisville School of Dentistry for their partnership and collaboration.

AUTHOR BIOGRAPHY

Jamie R. Abrams is a Professor of Law teaching torts, family law, legislation, legal writing, and women and the law. She teaches at the University of Louisville Brandeis School of Law. She has authored numerous articles about tort law and legal education pedagogy that inform her approach to this book.

From 2015–2018, she authored the KENTUCKY TORTS PRACTICE SERIES legal treatise updates. She authored the Historical Commentary on *Tarasoff v. Regents of the University of California* in FEMINIST JUDGMENTS: REWRITTEN TORT OPINIONS (M. Chamallas & L. M. Finley ed., Cambridge University Press) (2020). She has also published tort law articles such as *The Illusion of Autonomy in Women's Medical Decision-Making*, 42 FLORIDA STATE L. REV. 17 (2015), *Distorted and Diminished Tort Claims for Women*, 34 CARDOZO L. REV. 1955 (2013) (reprinted in Women and the Law (Tracy Thomas ed. 2014)), and *From Barbarity to Regularity: A Comparative Case Study of "Unnecesarean" Malpractice Claims*, 63 S.C. L. REV. 191 (2011). She has also published widely in the areas of feminist theory, masculinities theory, immigrant justice, and reproductive rights.

Professor Abrams is a national leader in legal education pedagogy reforms. She has published pedagogy articles such as *The Deconstructed Law School Exam,* 68 J. OF LEGAL EDUC. 194 (Winter 2019), *Experiential Learning and Assessment in the Era of Donald Trump*, 55 DUQUESNE UNIV. L. REV. 75 (2017), *Reframing the Socratic Method*, 64 J. OF LEGAL EDUC. 562 (2015), and *A Synergistic Pedagogical Approach to First-Year Teaching*, 48 DUQ. UNIV. L. REV. 423 (2010).

Professor Abrams was awarded the University of Louisville Brandeis School of Law's Teacher of the Year Award in 2016. She received the University of Louisville's Presidential Multicultural Teaching Award in 2014 for her demonstrated commitment to teaching, research, and service that integrate diverse perspectives. She also received the 2011 Innovations in Teaching Award from the American University Washington College of Law for her work spearheading an integrated curriculum skills simulation for 1Ls. She was awarded the Mussey-Gillett Shining Star Award from the District of Columbia's Women's Bar Association for her work co-authoring reports on the status of women and women of color in the legal profession as part of the WBA's nationally recognized Initiative on Advancement and Retention of Women.

Before entering law teaching, she worked as a Litigation Associate at Willkie Farr & Gallagher LLP where she specialized in complex civil litigation matters, including accounting malpractice and products liability cases. She received her LL.M from Columbia University and her J.D. from the American University Washington College of Law, receiving the highest academic honors from both institutions. She received her B.A. from Indiana University-Bloomington.

TABLE OF CONTENTS

ACKNOWLEDGMENTS III

AUTHOR BIOGRAPHY V

Introduction 1

Chapter 1. Intentional Torts 3
I.   Introduction 3
II.   Police Report 5
III.   News Article 6
IV.   Diagram of Gun Range 7
V.   Employee Affidavit 8
VI.   Legal Research 9
        (A) Procedural Rules 9
        (B) Practice Guidance 9
VII.   The Simulation Exercise 16

Chapter 2. Negligence: Standard of Care 17
I.   Introduction 17
II.   Sam Kennedy: Client Intake Memorandum 19
III.   Sam Kennedy: New Client Intake Form 20
IV.   Affidavit of Treating Physician Morgan 21
V.   Affidavit of Treating Physician Salyer 22
VI.   Stipulation of Facts 23
VII.   Plaintiff's Expert Retainer Agreement 24
VIII.   Defendant's Expert Retainer Agreement 26
IX.   Deposition Practice Guidelines 27
X.   The Simulation Exercise 28

Chapter 3. Negligence: Causation 29
I.   Introduction 29
II.   Discovery Document Production 31
III.   Website Excerpt 32
IV.   Online Product Reviews 33
V.   Model Causation Jury Instructions 34
VI.   The Simulation Exercise 35

Chapter 4. Negligence: Duty of Care 37
I.   Introduction 37
II.   Wife's Text 39
III.   Wife's Affidavit 40
IV.   Legal Research 41
        (A) Procedural Rules 41
        (B) Substantive Law 41
V.   The Simulation Exercise 49

Chapter 5. Negligence: Damages 51
I.   Introduction 51
II.   Journal of Sam Kennedy 52
III.   Billing Records 54

IV.   The Simulation Exercise 61

Chapter 6. Owners and Occupiers of Land Liability **63**
I.   Introduction 63
II.   Interview Notes 64
III.   Legal Research 67
IV.   The Simulation Exercise 68

Chapter 7. Wrongful Death and Survival **69**
I.   Introduction 69
II.   Supporting Documents 71
III.   Legal Research 82
       (A) Substantive Law 82
       (B) Practice Guidance 83
IV.   The Simulation Exercise 87

Chapter 8. Products Liability **89**
I.   Introduction 89
II.   Product Description 92
III.   Online Product Reviews 93
IV.   Deposition Excerpt 94
V.   Legal Research 95
       (A) Substantive Law 95
            (1) Restatement Provisions 95
            (2) Risk Utility Factors 95
       (B) Procedural Rules 96
VI.   The Simulation Exercise 97

Chapter 9. Defenses **99**
I.   Introduction 99
II.   Police Report 100
III.   Legal Research 101
       (A) Substantive Law 101
       (B) Procedural Rules 101
       (C) Practice Guidance 103
IV.   The Simulation Exercise 105

Chapter 10. Joint Tortfeasors **107**
I.   Introduction 107
II.   Client E-Mail 110
III.   Legal Research 111
IV.   The Simulation Exercise 112

Chapter 11. Strict Liability **113**
I.   Introduction 113
II.   Local News Story 115
III.   Meeting Inquiry 116
IV.   Fracking Background Research 116
V.   Corporate Web Site Excerpt 118
VI.   Legal Research 119
       (A) Substantive Law 119
       (B) Procedural Rules 119
VII.   The Simulation Exercise 120

Chapter 12. Defamation..**121**
I.   Introduction 121
II.   Website Reviews 123
III.   Correspondence..125
IV.   Legal Research..126
V.   The Simulation Exercise..127

TORT LAW SIMULATIONS

INTRODUCTION

Traditional casebooks introduce tort law using edited appellate cases with neat and tidy facts, moving across various jurisdictions and historical time periods, and only lightly addressing the underlying lawyering considerations. This approach—on its own—is highly imperfect. It is like starting a movie near its ending without careful development of the characters and without experiencing the viewer's initial uncertainty and suspense as to where the plot will take you. The end of the movie, like an appellate opinion, is focused on tying up the story neatly and completely. This approach loses sight of how legal cases begin with undefined issues and facts. Clients do not walk into your office with clear tort cases at all, let alone walk in with a negligence case with facts laid out succinctly and precisely. Clients walk in with harms and vulnerabilities that the lawyer unravels and resolves methodically over years.

This simulation book works to fill the gaps left by a traditional case-based instructional method. It magnifies the full and complex human realities that bring a tort case to life. A lawsuit begins years before the neat and tidy appellate case when an injured party suffers harm, perhaps life-altering harm, so substantial as to hire a lawyer and seek compensation.

Even before the case gets filed, threshold questions of access to justice fester. In what communities are lawyers abundantly advertising for business and readily accessible to potential clients? For which harms do lawyers advertise and market their practices? Which communities are left under-represented in the economic models of tort law client-generation? What types of preventable harms are not even yet understood as actionable torts?

On the other side of the "v.", a lawsuit begins with a defendant presented with financial risk, reputational threats, and great personal or professional uncertainty. Defendants might spend years defending a case successfully. While the defendant might win in the end, might the reputational harms and financial costs have been catastrophic anyway? Embedded in every tort case might be great financial upheaval, emotion, harm, disruption, risk, regret, and loss for all parties. This book brings these lawyering complexities to life with a series of simulation exercises representing plaintiffs and defendants at various stages in litigation.

This simulation book builds upon your traditional tort law casebook to help you "bridge to practice." It urges you to wrestle with the messiness and costs of ascertaining facts, the uncertainty of advising clients, and the potential disconnect between the depths of the losses suffered and the limited compensatory and punitive remedies available through civil suits. This text is designed to accompany the rigorous acquisition of doctrinal rules in a first-year class to prepare you for the modern realities of tort law practice.

Tort law is a particularly dynamic and accessible subject matter to prepare students for the practice of law. You can pick up nearly any newspaper on any day and see the impact of tort law all around you. Tort law is all around us shaping the norms that drive our behaviors and our interactions with others. It is tort law that might give you pause before texting and driving or drinking that hot cup of coffee. Tort law is also powerfully community-based in its rules. Communities might differ from city to city and town to town, for example, in their views about what a "reasonable" belief of danger to life or limb might be. Each community's norms might change over time in response to political, social, economic, and moral factors. Communities might differ dramatically in their views about regulations, state action, obligations to others, property protections, and more. Tort law is thus a powerful subject matter to keep your peripheral vision wide open to the world around you as these norms change over time in your community.

Tort law is also uniquely versatile. It has historically filled gaps in law and regulation before other legal regimes later emerge, such as historically addressing harms we now think of as sexual harassment, environmental law, and health and safety standards. As the COVID-19 virus swept the nation in a global pandemic, it was tort waivers of liability first deployed to manage risks. Companies were incentivized to comply with published health guidelines knowing that their compliance might protect them from tort liability. Tort law filled gaps and shaped behaviors in the face of great uncertainty well before legislation was feasible or likely.

The organization of typical torts casebooks gives the impression of boundaries and silos. You study intentional torts, and then you leave it behind. You study negligence, and then you move on. This book breaks these artificial boundaries, allowing the field of tort law to take shape for you. It catapults you into law practice in your first semesters of law school, rather than creating an artificial line between the study of tort law and the practice of tort law.

This book uses modern fictional simulations of current events to apply torts concepts to the most complex pressing modern problems. It intentionally avoids "neat and tidy" cases. It opts instead for complex modern socio-legal problems that you might encounter in practice.

This book is generally organized around two separate client simulations. The first simulation develops tragic facts that take place at a gun range. You will work with this simulation in your units on intentional torts, wrongful death, owners and occupiers, duty of care, defenses, and defamation. This simulation reveals how textbook units interconnect and how tort lawyers consider multiple possible defendants and multiple possible claims. The facts of this simulation may be rawer and more complex for certain communities struggling with the traumas of gun violence. I reflected on that hardship carefully. I acknowledge that complexity deeply as an author. I ultimately concluded though that these contested social norms and raw community emotions are exactly where tort law reveals itself in such interesting and dynamic ways. Different juries might reach different conclusions based on the same facts and the same law in light of their unique community perspectives in that exact social, political, and economic moment. Tort law might be exactly the site where we first observe legal norms changing well before legislative action on controversial, emotional, and divisive issues.

The second simulation involves a dental injury that a patient suffered after a root canal. While it is less controversial in its subject matter, it strikes a different sort of nerve! Again, it challenges us to consider how plaintiffs navigate multiple defendants and multiple claims. The simulation develops throughout chapters unpacking the standards of care, causation, and damages elements of negligence. It also continues into products liability, joint tortfeasors, and defamation.

These simulations also empower you to work with research sources far beyond the typical 1L appellate cases. The exercises incorporate statutes into your understanding of tort law. They demonstrate how secondary sources and practitioner tools can save valuable time and resources for lawyers performing new tasks in their careers.

These simulations are primarily designed to apply substantive tort law, but they also go much further to demonstrate how law practice seamlessly connects procedure, substance, and strategy. The exercises help you see how civil procedure maps on to tort claims. These simulations include complaint drafting, client meetings, discovery drafting, damage calculations, depositions, settlement demands, and more. They help you see the value of comprehensive legal research and strong writing and reasoning skills. They show the value of thoughtful case strategy, reasoned judgment, and refined professionalism in law practice.

Legal education is changing rapidly. I hope that these simulations bring your torts studies alive in challenging and empowering ways; bring greater clarity and mastery to the legal concepts; and bridge the study of law into the exciting and dynamic practice of law.

CHAPTER 1

INTENTIONAL TORTS

I. INTRODUCTION

Most tort law courses begin with the intentional torts unit. This is a tricky place for students to start. Many students come to law school conceptualizing the field of torts around medical malpractice, car accidents, and slip and fall cases. Students have seen the law firm billboards in their hometowns advertising client representation for these types of negligence injuries. Never do you see a law firm billboard advertising for trespass or false imprisonment cases. Some intentional tort causes of action can also seem similar to criminal law content, which many students might be taking simultaneously and find confusing to disentangle.

Intentional torts is also a fast-paced unit in which students progress from one cause of action to another often learning a new tort every single class. This stands in stark contrast to negligence, which occupies the bulk of the semester unfolding over weeks and weeks.

The sooner you can apply intentional torts concepts, the more likely you will master and embrace this material. Through application exercises, you can see how claims relate to each other and how they allow plaintiffs to recover for their harms. In this chapter, you will apply all of your intentional torts material to a client simulation. It replicates the issue-spotting and client intake that lawyers do in practice.

Students analyzing intentional torts issues need to first apply the intent standard to all intentional torts. This is often the hardest part of this unit. Intent requires that the tortfeasor intended to do the act, not that the tortfeasor intended the harmful consequences of the act. Teaching this rule always reminds me of negotiating squabbles among my children. Inevitably one of my children will make a move or gesture—let's say tickling their sibling—that is intended to be playful, funny, or gentle, but nonetheless has the effect of hurting my other child as he falls off the couch, for example. The offender child will plead with me that they "didn't mean to hurt their sibling." That, however, is not the question for the purposes of intentional tort law. Focusing just on intent, without any other intentional tort elements, the question is whether the offender child intended to tickle her sibling. If so, she is liable for the harms that the act caused. If, instead, the sibling lost her footing and tripped, knocking her sibling down, then there would be no intent there because she did not intend to do the act.

The next step to intentional torts analysis involves layering the intent element on to the rest of the intentional tort elements for battery, assault, false imprisonment, intentional infliction of emotional distress, trespass, trespass to chattel, and conversion. Rigor and precision in factual application is key here. Lawyers should precisely state the elements of an intentional tort and then identify facts proving that each element has been met. As you read the primary cases assigned in your casebook, you should extract the elements for each intentional tort.

This simulation then positions you to practice applying these elements from your casebook to a new set of facts, just as a lawyer would do in practice. You will read the subsequent case file materials as a plaintiff's lawyer. In other chapters you will role play as defense counsel. You will use this case file for later chapters on duty, wrongful death, owners and occupiers, and defamation. The case materials are first introduced partially and preliminarily in this chapter simulating how a case begins with limited facts and information. This case file develops further in later chapters. It is a quite difficult and upsetting sequence of events that left many parties harmed physically and emotionally. The practice of tort law likewise involves working with clients in their most vulnerable moments during great hardship and suffering.

You will sift through these facts to identify which plaintiffs have viable claims to be pursued in a civil case. Note the difference between working with this simulation and studying cases from your primary casebook. When you open your tort law casebook, you already know from the headings and the chapters that the case you are about to read must involve a tort → intentional tort → battery. In the practice of law, an injured party enters your law practice with no such headings or clarity. It is your job to figure out whether the client's injuries are torts at all, whether they are intentional torts or negligence, and whether they raise claims for battery or assault.

There are multiple causes of action arising from this case file. You will examine a news story, a police report, a diagram of the premises, and an employee affidavit to identify intentional tort causes of action. While you are reading a police report from a potential criminal case, remember that we are working to tear down the artificial silos that separate your first-year courses. The police report would surely trigger criminal charges, but it might also be strong evidence of civil claims as well.

Your assignment is to draft a complaint initiating a civil suit for damages by injured parties. The standard for pleading a complaint will be provided to you. It is a critical task for tort lawyers to draft complaints effectively. The complaint initiates the lawsuit and begins the process of obtaining discovery to learn more about the facts of the case. Complaint drafting is an early litigation stage in which plaintiffs' lawyers only know their clients' side of the story and some preliminary facts. Lawyers need to include enough facts in the complaint to prove that they could meet each element of the cause of action, while acknowledging that there are more facts to be discovered as the case proceeds.

———————————

II. POLICE REPORT

Case No: 294850-398494   **Date:** March 4

Reporting Officer: Officer Clayton Brown   **Prepared By:** Officer Clayton Brown

Incident: Shooting accident at Sharp Shooter's Gun Range, killing a male patron on impact, injuring a female patron—ultimately leading to her death days later, and injuring two more patrons.

Detail of Event:

On March 4, Harold Husband went to the Sharp Shooter's Gun Range at approximately 11 a.m. to engage in target shooting. While at the range, he received a text message from his wife, Wendy, at 11:43 a.m. stating, "I know you R @ the range. Sorry to do this by text, I knew you would lose it when I told you. I'm divorcing U." Ervin Employee said he heard Harold Husband start crying and muttering things like "I cannot go on without her" and "how could she do this?" Ervin Employee then saw Harold Husband take his gun and fire it repeatedly in the air, not directly at any patrons.

One of the shots hit Damien Dagger, a patron at Sharp Shooter's, in the head and killed him immediately on impact with no warning. Another shot hit Molly May in the left side of her chest. Gertrude Guest and Ervin Employee hid behind the wooden barrier between Harold's lane and Gertrude's lane trying to protect themselves. Two of the bullets pierced the wooden barrier between lanes, injuring Gertrude Guest in the arm and Ervin Employee in the leg. Will Witness jumped on the back of Harold Husband after a few shots were fired, restraining him until the police arrived.

Actions Taken:

When I arrived at the scene, I arrested Harold and removed the gun. He complained of pain in his shoulder and was escorted in an ambulance to the hospital with Officer Hobbes. I observed the deceased body of Damien Dagger. Molly May was taken to the hospital in the first ambulance, as she was non-responsive. Ervin Employee and Gertrude Guest were taken in the ambulances that arrived later.

I recovered the phone of Harold Husband, along with the semi-automatic weapon involved in the accident. He had rented this weapon from the facility. There was also a bag belonging to Harold Husband containing his wallet.

There were marks on the ceiling of the gun range, and holes in the wooden partitions separating lanes on both the right and left sides. Broken glass from lights that had been shattered was also on the ground.

Will Witness was uninjured. He stated that while shooting he saw a light shatter and heard people screaming. He located where Harold was shooting wildly in the air and brought him down to the ground.

I then went to the hospital to interview witnesses. Molly May was in critical condition. Ervin Employee required 12 stitches in the leg. Gertrude Guest required surgery for a shattered bone in her arm. Harold Husband had a separated shoulder from contact with Will Witness. [Upon later investigation, Molly May died two days later from her gunshot wound. Gertrude Guest is in therapy for Post-Traumatic Stress Disorder and night terrors.]

III. NEWS ARTICLE

WIFE TEXTS FOR DIVORCE, HUSBAND SHOOTS FOUR

March 7, 6:34 a.m. - Harold Husband and Wendy Wife had been married six years when she sent a text message that would soon change countless lives forever - a message seeking a divorce. In a fit of emotion, Harold Husband shot seven rounds into the air, killing two and injuring two more. When the police arrived, a disgruntled Harold Husband was being detained by a patron.

Harold, while having no criminal history of violence, does have a history of anger management issues. Not only had he recently started anger management classes, but a family friend reported that his wife had made these classes a condition of her staying in the relationship with him. The family friend, who wished to remain anonymous, stated that often times Wendy Wife was scared to disagree with Harold because he tended to scream and to overreact in rage.

The arresting officer, Officer Clayton Brown, reported: "Harold was crying and in shock at the scene, sobbing that 'he never meant to hurt anyone.' He seems to have panicked and shot in the air."

Representatives of Sharp Shooter's Gun Range say that the facility will be closed until further notice to allow their employees time to cope.

IV. DIAGRAM OF GUN RANGE

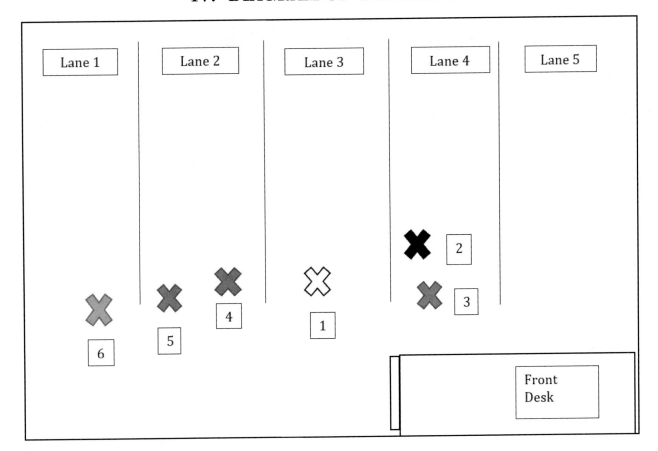

Sharp Shooter's Gun Range – Police Diagram

Key:

1 – Harold Husband
2 – Ervin Employee
3 – Gertrude Guest
4 – Damien Dagger
5 – Molly May
6 – Will Witness

V. EMPLOYEE AFFIDAVIT

VOLUNTARY STATEMENT

Ervin Employee

Name

Sharp Shooter's Gun Range   Employee

Place of Work   Role

5339 Pistol Drive, Tortsylvania 12345   293-268-0000

Address

Phone

I, <u>Ervin Employee</u>, hereby make the following statement:

On March 4, I was working the day shift at Sharp Shooter's Gun Range. A man came into the range. He'd been here before. His name was Harold Husband. He was in a good mood and I checked him into Lane 3. He rented a gun for use. I was helping Gertrude Guest with the magazine of the gun she had rented. I heard Harold Husband, who was in the adjacent lane to where I was with Gertrude, slam his fist in the side wall of his lane. I was uneasy. He started sobbing uncontrollably and said "I can't live without her" and "how could she?" This went on for about one minute when he slammed his fist on the side partition again, and shots began going off. I had Gertrude get down beside me. We were terrified. We hid next to the side of the lane wall. A shot came through the side wall and hit Gertrude's arm. About that time a shot came through the wall and hit my leg, tearing my pants. I heard footsteps and a large thud. A male voice yelled for everyone to stay where they were, and that the shooter was down, but not to move. About five minutes later, the police and EMS arrived. I spent two days in the hospital.

I swear (or affirm) that the information in the statement above is true to the best of my knowledge or belief.

Ervin Employee   March 8   9:30 am

(Witness' Signature)   (Date)   Time

Sworn to and subscribed before me on this date.

Clayton Brown   March 8   9:30 am

(Investigator's Signature)   (Date)   Time

VI. LEGAL RESEARCH

(A) PROCEDURAL RULES

Below are short excerpts from the Federal Rules of Civil Procedure. These rules advise you how to style a complaint for relief. These rules can be used to structure the preceding facts into a complaint. They also inform your brainstorming of what facts present viable causes of action and what claims fall short. These are both federal procedural rules that would govern in federal court. In civil procedure you will study whether a lawsuit will be filed in federal or state court. Tort lawsuits will often be state cases applying state rules of civil procedure. The federal rules are used for this simulation exercise because they likely reinforce your civil procedure course content.

Rule 8. General Rules of Pleading

(a)   Claim for Relief. A pleading that states a claim for relief must contain:

(1)   a short and plain statement of the grounds for the court's jurisdiction, unless the court already has jurisdiction and the claim needs no new jurisdictional support;

(2)   a short and plain statement of the claim showing that the pleader is entitled to relief; and

(3)   a demand for the relief sought, which may include relief in the alternative or different types of relief.

Rule 10. Form of Pleadings

(a)   Caption; Names of Parties. Every pleading must have a caption with the court's name, a title, [and] a file number. . . The title of the complaint must name all the parties; the title of other pleadings, after naming the first party on each side, may refer generally to other parties.

(b)   Paragraphs; Separate Statements. A party must state its claims or defenses in numbered paragraphs, each limited as far as practicable to a single set of circumstances. A later pleading may refer by number to a paragraph in an earlier pleading.

(B) PRACTICE GUIDANCE

You have never drafted a civil complaint before. You thus research some practice materials to save you valuable time and resources. You find the following civil complaint for battery, assault, and intentional infliction of emotional distress. This suit was brought against a security guard and the security company that employed him. The entity can also be held liable for the actions of its employees. You will study this concept further in your casebook materials on vicarious liability. For this simulation, the excerpt contains only pleadings in the alternatives for intentional torts against the individual defendant.

Practitioner guidances like these are a good starting point. Your law practice may have its own templates and forms generated for your use as well. Samples and templates are only a starting point though. Lawyers need to carefully customize and style a new complaint for each lawsuit. It is a precise and tedious task.

2012 WL 12850389 (Cal.Super.) (Trial Pleading)
Superior Court of California.
Los Angeles County

Timothy Cameron DEWITT (aka T.C. Dewitt), an individual; Plaintiff,

v.

GENERAL SECURITY SERVICE, INC., a business organization, form unknown;
Edmond Mushegyan, an individual; New Vision Assets, Inc.
(sued as Doe 91); John Stewart Company (sued as Doe 92);
and Does 1 to 200, Inclusive; Defendants.

No. BC470993.
October 17, 2012.

**Verified Third Amended Complaint for Assault; Battery; False Imprisonment;
Negligent Infliction of Emotional Distress; Intentional
Infliction of Emotional Distress; Negligence**

COMES NOW, TIMOTHY CAMERON DEWITT (aka T.C. DEWITT), who alleges as follows:

GENERAL ALLEGATIONS

1. Plaintiff, TIMOTHY CAMERON DEWITT, aka T.C. DEWITT (hereinafter "Plaintiff"), is an individual, and at all relevant times mentioned in this complaint, was a resident of Los Angeles County, California.

2. Plaintiff is informed and believes, and on the basis of that information and belief alleges, that Defendant GENERAL SECURITY SERVICE, INC. is a business organization, form unknown, which at all times mentioned in this complaint, maintained a business address in Los Angeles County, California.

3. Plaintiff is informed and believes, and on the basis of that information and belief alleges, that Defendant EDMOND MUSHEGYAN is an individual, and is now, and at all times mentioned in this complaint was, a resident of Los Angeles County, California. Plaintiff is informed and believes, and on the basis of that information and belief alleges, that on or about October 12, 2009, Defendants EDMOND MUSHEGYAN and DOES 1 to 15, Inclusive (hereinafter collectively "MUSHEGYAN") were employees or agents of Defendant GENERAL SECURITY SERVICE, INC., and DOES 10 to 200, Inclusive. * * *

6. Plaintiff is informed and believes and thereon alleges that at all times herein mentioned each of the defendants was the agent and employee of each of the remaining defendants, and in doing the things hereinafter alleged, each defendant was acting within the course and scope of such agency.

EVENTS OCCURRING ON OR ABOUT OCTOBER 12, 2009

7. On or about October 12, 2009, Plaintiff lawfully parked the vehicle he was driving (hereinafter "the vehicle") on Las Palmas Boulevard, between Franklin Avenue and Hollywood Boulevard, in the City of Los Angeles, California. Plaintiff left the vehicle for a short period of time, and for a while, the vehicle was out of Plaintiff's line of sight.

8. While returning to the vehicle, and upon re-gaining sight of the vehicle, Plaintiff noticed that the cab and bed lights of the vehicle were illuminated. Upon returning to the vehicle, Plaintiff encountered MUSHEGYAN leaning into Plaintiff's vehicle through the passenger side. The passenger door of the vehicle was now open.

9. In an apparent reaction to Plaintiff's use of reasonable force to protect the vehicle, MUSHEGYAN drew a gun from his person. MUSHEGYAN, pointed the gun at Plaintiff's chest, causing Plaintiff to fear injury and to fear for his life. MUSHEGYAN, was approximately one (1) to five (5) feet from Plaintiff at this time.

10. Plaintiff slowly backed away from MUSHEGYAN. MUSHEGYAN advanced on Plaintiff, maintaining a distance of approximately one (1) to five (5) feet from Plaintiff. MUSHEGYAN also pushed the tip of the gun into Plaintiff's chest.

11. Plaintiff eventually was able to enter the driver's side of the vehicle, and seated himself in the driver's seat of the vehicle. Plaintiff attempted to drive away from the scene, without further incident. Plaintiff is informed and believes, and based upon this information and belief alleges, that while Plaintiff attempted to drive away from the scene, without further incident, MUSHEGYAN remained at or near the rear of where the vehicle had been parked. * * *

FIRST CAUSE OF ACTION

Assault

By Plaintiff Against Defendants EDMOND MUSHEGYAN, GENERAL SECURITY SERVICE, INC., and DOES 1 to 200, Inclusive.

14. Plaintiff re-alleges and incorporates by reference the allegations in Paragraphs 1 through 13 of this Complaint, as though set forth in full.

15. On or about October 12, 2009, MUSHEGYAN placed Plaintiff in fear of a harmful or offensive conduct, including by drawing a gun from MUSHEGYAN'S person, pointing the gun at Plaintiff's chest, threatening to shoot Plaintiff with the gun, and firing at least two shots at Plaintiff with the gun, one of which Plaintiff is informed and believes became lodged in the vehicle while Plaintiff was seated in the driver's seat of the vehicle, attempting to drive away from the scene without further incident.

16. Plaintiff reasonably believed that he was about to be touched in a harmful or offensive manner by MUSHEGYAN.

17. Plaintiff is informed and believes, and based upon this information and belief alleges, that in doing the acts as alleged above, MUSHEGYAN intended to cause, or to place Plaintiff in apprehension of, a harmful or an offensive contact with Plaintiff's person.

18. Based upon the actions of MUSHEGYAN, including drawing a gun from Defendant MUSHEGYAN'S person, pointing the gun at Plaintiff's chest, threatening to shoot Plaintiff with the gun, and shooting the gun at Plaintiff, it reasonably appeared to Plaintiff that MUSHEGYAN was about to carry out the threat.

19. At no time did Plaintiff consent to any of the acts of MUSHEGYAN, as alleged above.

20. As a proximate result of the acts of MUSHEGYAN, as alleged above, Plaintiff was hurt and injured in his strength, and activity, sustaining injury to his nervous system and person, all of which have caused, and continue to cause, Plaintiff great mental, physical and nervous pain and suffering.

21. As a further proximate result of the acts of MUSHEGYAN, Plaintiff has incurred, and will continue to incur, medical and related expenses. The full amount of these expenses is not known to Plaintiff at this time. Plaintiff will move to amend this Complaint to state the amount if, and when, it becomes known to him, or on proof thereof.

22. As a further proximate result of the acts of MUSHEGYAN, Plaintiff was prevented from attending to his usual occupation and his writing and entertainment career, and impaired in such activities for an as yet undetermined period. Plaintiff thereby has lost and will lose earnings in an as yet ascertained amount. Plaintiff will seek to amend this Complaint, if, and when, such amount is ascertained.

23. As a further proximate result of the acts of MUSHEGYAN, Plaintiff's present and future earning capacity has been greatly impaired. The exact amount of this loss is not known to Plaintiff

at this time, and Plaintiff will move to amend this Complaint to state the amount if, and when, it becomes known to him, or on proof thereof.

24. As a further proximate result of the acts of MUSHEGYAN, Plaintiff's quality of life has been severely impacted because, for example, Plaintiff lives in fear of similar trauma; Plaintiff can no longer fully enjoy many activities which Plaintiff greatly appreciated prior to the events of October 12, 2009, including but not limited to, drawing, acting, and running.

25. Plaintiff is informed and believes, and on the basis of that information and belief alleges, that the acts of MUSHEGYAN, as herein alleged, were willful, wanton, malicious, and oppressive, and justify the awarding of punitive damages. * * *

SECOND CAUSE OF ACTION

Battery

By Plaintiff Against Defendant EDMOND MUSHEGYAN, GENERAL SECURITY SERVICE, INC., and DOES 1 to 200, Inclusive.

40. Plaintiff re-alleges and incorporates by reference the allegations in Paragraphs 1 through 39 of this Complaint, as though set forth in full.

41. On or about October 12, 2009, MUSHEGYAN touched Plaintiff, or caused Plaintiff to be touched, with the intent to harm or offend Plaintiff, including by pushing the tip of a gun into Plaintiff's chest; and firing at least two shots at Plaintiff with the gun, one of which Plaintiff is informed and believes became lodged in the vehicle, while another bullet struck Plaintiff in the head, and the bullet traveled into Plaintiff's brain—all gun shots fired at Plaintiff by MUSHEGYAN on or about October 12, 2009, were fired as Plaintiff attempted to drive away from the scene, without further incident.

42. At no time did Plaintiff consent to any of the acts of MUSHEGYAN, as alleged above.

43. As a proximate result of the acts of MUSHEGYAN, as alleged above, Plaintiff was hurt and injured in his strength, and activity, sustaining injury to his nervous system and person, all of which have caused, and continue to cause, Plaintiff great mental, physical and nervous pain and suffering. For example, as a proximate result of the acts of MUSHEGYAN, Plaintiff is partially blind, as Plaintiff's brain is unable to process the left field of vision from either eye; Plaintiff had nineteen (19) staples attached to his head for a period of time; a metal plate was inserted into Plaintiff's head at the entry point of the bullet to partially remedy the partial destruction of his skull.

44. As a further proximate result of the acts of MUSHEGYAN, Plaintiff has incurred, and will continue to incur, medical and related expenses. The full amount of these expenses is not known to Plaintiff at this time. Plaintiff will move to amend this Complaint to state the amount if, and when, it becomes known to him, or on proof thereof.

45. As a further proximate result of the acts of MUSHEGYAN, Plaintiff was prevented from attending to his usual occupation as a projection manager and his writing and entertainment career, and impaired in such activities for an as yet undetermined period. Plaintiff thereby has lost and will lose earnings in an as yet ascertained amount. Plaintiff will seek to amend this Complaint, if, and when, such amount is ascertained.

46. As a further proximate result of the acts of MUSHEGYAN, Plaintiff's present and future earning capacity has been greatly impaired. The exact amount of this loss is not known to Plaintiff at this time, and Plaintiff will move to amend this Complaint to state the amount if, and when, it becomes known to him, or on proof thereof.

47. As a further proximate result of the acts of MUSHEGYAN, Plaintiff's quality of life has been severely impacted because, for example, Plaintiff lives in fear of similar trauma; Plaintiff can no longer fully enjoy many activities which Plaintiff greatly appreciated prior to the events of October

12, 2009, including but not limited to, drawing, acting, and running; Plaintiff can no longer drive, and is forced to endure public transportation, or ask others to chauffeur him to his destination; there are numerous other activities and daily functions Plaintiff can no longer perform, either at all, or to the standards he could ordinarily meet prior to October 12, 2009; Plaintiff is precluded from applying for many employment opportunities; Plaintiff struggles in crowds, and suffers from anxiety when in groups; Plaintiff suffers from periodic migraines and numbness on parts of his body.

48. Plaintiff is informed and believes, and on the basis of that information and belief alleges, that the acts of MUSHEGYAN, as herein alleged, were willful, wanton, malicious, and oppressive, and justify the awarding of punitive damages. * * *

THIRD CAUSE OF ACTION

False Imprisonment

By Plaintiff Against Defendants EDMOND MUSHEGYAN, GENERAL SECURITY SERVICE, INC., and DOES 1 to 200, Inclusive.

63. Plaintiff re-alleges and incorporates by reference the allegations in Paragraphs 1 through 62 of this Complaint, as though set forth in full.

64. On or about October 12, 2009, MUSHEGYAN intentionally deprived Plaintiff of his freedom of movement by use of physical barriers, force, threats of force, menace, fraud, deceit, and unreasonable duress.

65. Immediately prior to the acts of MUSHEGYAN, Plaintiff had been peacefully returning to his vehicle, which was lawfully parked on Las Palmas Boulevard, between Franklin Avenue and Hollywood Boulevard, in the City of Los Angeles, California. Plaintiff did not steal, nor was he in the process of stealing, any property, nor had he committed any crime against MUSHEGYAN, or anyone else. Plaintiff is informed and believes, and on the basis of that information and belief alleges, that MUSHEGYAN knew, or should have known, of Plaintiff's innocence.

66. The confinement of Plaintiff by MUSHEGYAN compelled Plaintiff to stay for some appreciable time.

67. Plaintiff did not knowingly or voluntarily consent to the confinement by MUSHEGYAN.

68. As a proximate result of the acts of MUSHEGYAN, Plaintiff was injured in his health, strength and activity, sustaining injury to his body, and shock and injury to his nervous system and person.

69. As a further proximate result of the acts of MUSHEGYAN, Plaintiff was required to and did employ physicians and surgeons for medical examination, treatment, and care of these injuries, and did incur medical and incidental expenses.

70. As a further proximate result of the acts of MUSHEGYAN, Plaintiff has incurred, and will incur, further medical and incidental expenses for the care and treatment of these injuries, the exact amount of which is unknown at this time.

71. As a further proximate result of the acts of MUSHEGYAN, Plaintiff was prevented from attending to his usual occupation as a projection manager and his writing and entertainment career, and impaired in such activities for an as yet undetermined period. Plaintiff thereby has lost and will lose earnings in an as yet ascertained amount. Plaintiff will seek to amend this Complaint, if, and when, such amount is ascertained.

72. Plaintiff is informed and believes, and on the basis of that information and belief alleges, that the acts of MUSHEGYAN, as herein alleged, were willful, wanton, malicious, and oppressive, and justify the awarding of punitive damages. * * *

FIFTH CAUSE OF ACTION

Intentional Infliction of Emotional Distress

By Plaintiff Against Defendant EDMOND MUSHEGYAN, GENERAL SECURITY SERVICE, INC., and DOES 1 to 200, Inclusive.

104. Plaintiff re-alleges and incorporates by reference the allegations in Paragraphs 1 through 103 of this Complaint, as though set forth in full.

105. Plaintiff is informed and believes, and on the basis of that information and belief alleges, that the aforementioned acts of MUSHEGYAN were outrageous.

106. Plaintiff is informed and believes, and on the basis of that information and belief alleges, that, in committing the aforementioned acts, MUSHEGYAN intended to cause Plaintiff emotional distress.

107. Plaintiff is informed and believes, and on the basis of that information and belief alleges, that, in committing the aforementioned acts, MUSHEGYAN acted with reckless disregard of the probability that Plaintiff would suffer emotional distress, knowing that Plaintiff was present when the conduct occurred.

108. As a proximate result of the aforementioned acts of MUSHEGYAN, Plaintiff suffered severe emotional distress.

109. As a proximate result of the acts of MUSHEGYAN, as alleged above, Plaintiff was hurt and injured in his strength, and activity, sustaining injury to his nervous system and person, all of which have caused, and continue to cause, Plaintiff great mental, physical and nervous pain and suffering.

110. As a further proximate result of the acts of MUSHEGYAN, Plaintiff has incurred, and will continue to incur, medical and related expenses. The full amount of these expenses is not known to Plaintiff at this time. Plaintiff will move to amend this Complaint to state the amount if, and when, it becomes known to him, or on proof thereof.

111. As a further proximate result of the acts of MUSHEGYAN, Plaintiff was prevented from attending to his usual occupation as a projection manager and his writing and entertainment career, and impaired in such activities for an as yet undetermined period. Plaintiff thereby has lost and will lose earnings in an as yet ascertained amount. Plaintiff will seek to amend this Complaint, if, and when, such amount is ascertained.

112. As a further proximate result of the acts of MUSHEGYAN, Plaintiff's present and future earning capacity has been greatly impaired. The exact amount of this loss is not known to Plaintiff at this time, and Plaintiff will move to amend this Complaint to state the amount if, and when, it becomes known to him, or on proof thereof.

113. As a further proximate result of the acts of MUSHEGYAN, Plaintiff's quality of life has been severely impacted because, for example, Plaintiff lives in fear of similar trauma; Plaintiff can no longer fully enjoy many activities which Plaintiff greatly appreciated prior to the events of October 12, 2009, including but not limited to, drawing, acting, and running.

114. Plaintiff is informed and believes, and on the basis of that information and belief alleges, that the acts of MUSHEGYAN, as herein alleged, were willful, wanton, malicious, and oppressive, and justify the awarding of punitive damages. * * *

WHEREFORE, Plaintiff prays for judgment against Defendants as follows:

ON THE FIRST CAUSE OF ACTION:

1.   For general damages, according to proof;

2.   For all medical and incidental expenses, according to proof;

3. For all loss of earnings, past and future, according to proof;

4. For punitive damages, according to proof;

5. For interest as allowed by law;

6. For costs of suit herein incurred; and

7. For such other and further relief as the Court may deem proper.

ON THE SECOND CAUSE OF ACTION:

1. For general damages, according to proof;

2. For all medical and incidental expenses, according to proof;

3. For all loss of earnings, past and future, according to proof;

4. For punitive damages, according to proof;

5. For interest as allowed by law;

6. For costs of suit herein incurred; and

7. For such other and further relief as the Court may deem proper.

ON THE THIRD CAUSE OF ACTION:

1. For general damages, according to proof;

2. For all medical and incidental expenses, according to proof;

3. For all loss of earnings, past and future, according to proof;

4. For punitive damages, according to proof;

5. For interest as allowed by law;

6. For costs of suit herein incurred; and

7. For such other and further relief as the Court may deem proper. * * *

ON THE FIFTH CAUSE OF ACTION:

1. For general damages, according to proof;

2. For all medical and incidental expenses, according to proof;

3. For all loss of earnings, past and future, according to proof;

4. For punitive damages, according to proof;

5. For interest as allowed by law;

6. For costs of suit herein incurred; and

7. For such other and further relief as the Court may deem proper.

VII. THE SIMULATION EXERCISE

The best way to master course concepts is to apply the substantive legal rules as real lawyers would. Here, you have just learned about a tragic set of events that transpired at Sharp Shooter's Gun Range. You will work to issue-spot the fact pattern thoroughly for all potential claims against possible intentional torts defendants just as a lawyer would do in practice.

Harold is the most obvious intentional tort defendant, but there may be others too. For issue-spotting, it might be helpful to first prepare a chart or an outline identifying who has viable causes of action, the elements to prove that cause of action, and the facts that support each element.

After preparing the list of potential claims, you will then style these claims into a complaint against Harold Husband (and any other potential defendants you identified) using the procedural rules above. In the complaint, address only intentional torts. State the elements of the claim and enough facts to prove that each element is met to comply with the Rule 8 procedural requirements. The sample complaint will help you visualize and conceptualize the task.

Do not consider negligence, strict liability, or any other legal theories.

Think carefully about how to manage pleading in the alternative. If you think that you have one successful intentional tort claim, should you include the others? What are the benefits and drawbacks of this? Try to organize your multiple causes of action strategically like a lawyer would. Consider which plaintiffs' injuries are most costly and which claims are strongest.

CHAPTER 2

NEGLIGENCE: STANDARD OF CARE

I. INTRODUCTION

The next four chapters develop each of the elements of negligence. The first building block to a negligence claim is identifying a breach in the standard of care. Without the plaintiff proving that the defendant breached a standard of care, the case cannot move on to causation or damages. Your casebook has introduced you to a variety of specialized standards of care, such as those governing children, persons with physical disabilities, persons with mental illness, and professionals. Some of these standards are modified to consider unique individualized traits of the defendant such as the standards governing children's conduct and physical disabilities. Other standards, such as mental illness, disregard the unique characteristics or conditions of the defendant.

Reading cases only from your casebook gives a distorted view of tort lawyering. It leaves the false impression that the facts and legal standards just "exist" in a case without revealing how much time, money, and lawyering went into a final published opinion in which the court simply states that the standard of care is X instead of Y.

The work of identifying what the standard of care is may be jury-intensive and costly. The plaintiff may need to argue to a jury that the defendant's conduct did not comport with what a reasonably prudent person would do under the same or similar circumstances. This can feel quite indeterminate to the parties wondering what a jury will conclude based on a particular set of facts.

Identifying the standard of care might alternatively involve introducing statutes as evidence of the standard of care under the negligence *per se* framework. If the statute is admitted, negligence *per se* can yield more predictable and fixed standards of care. Using statutes to fix standards of care then raises other pragmatic questions of human experience. Do you actually know the content of statutes to which you might be held accountable in tort law? What are the statutory rules for using electronic devices while driving, car maintenance, home maintenance, boater safety, home renovations, etc.? Would the statutes have passed the legislature if they explicitly included tort liability? Your home state might have a statute imposing a fine for texting and driving, for example, but as a practical matter, drivers still do it regularly. The legislature and community might have thought very differently about enacting that law if it said explicitly that its implications were both to impose a fine on violators and to impose potentially unlimited tort liability.

Identifying what the standard of care is might alternatively involve requesting evidentiary instructions allowing the jury to make inferences consistent with *res ipsa loquitur* or with circumstantial evidence case theories. These situations position the court as a gatekeeper determining whether a jury will be allowed to make inferences to support the plaintiff's argument that the defendant breached a standard of care. These cases requesting an evidentiary instruction to infer a standard of care reflect something of a last-ditch effort for a plaintiff's case to reach a jury.

Finally, identifying the standard of care may also require expert witnesses. In cases involving professional negligence, the case may involve experts reaching competing conclusions about what the standard of care is. This can significantly ratchet up the costs of litigation as both plaintiffs and defendants interview and retain competing experts. Those experts are then paid hourly to review the case files and to draw conclusions based on their training and subject matter expertise.

The foundation to this work involves taking and defending depositions in which experts testify as to their conclusions and findings. The plaintiff's expert will try to establish that the defendant's conduct breached a standard of care and caused the plaintiff's harm. The defendant's expert will try to establish that the defendant's conduct was within the governing standard of care and/or that it did not cause the plaintiff's harms. Depositions are often the vehicle for developing the standard of care using experts. Depositions provide a preview of what will come out at trial.

In this chapter, you will practice taking and defending depositions governing the applicable standard of care in a dental malpractice case. We will use these case file materials for several chapters. The case materials are first introduced in this chapter. The defendant in this case is a dentist who treated Sam Kennedy. The defendant has stipulated to some of the facts underlying the injuries the plaintiff suffered. Both the defendant and the plaintiff have hired experts to testify regarding the applicable standards of care.

The case file includes the notes that the plaintiff's lawyer took when first meeting the new client. Note that the lawyer is considering possible damage recoveries and brainstorming possible defendants from day one of the client intake. While it may be weeks before you discuss damages in your course, damages notably shape the case at the outset.

The case file also includes two affidavits of the other treating doctors stipulating to the facts of which they have knowledge in Sam's treatment after the initial surgery. These dentists are all fact witnesses. These statements focus the case for the parties. The parties notably agree on much of what happened to Sam Kennedy. They disagree on the legal significance of the defendant-dentist's conduct in that chain of events.

The case file also includes the competing retainer letters for each party's respective expert in the case. A retainer letter typically reveals each expert's substantive position on the case in broad strokes. The retainer letter is private to each party, so in practice each side would have only its own retainer letter, not both. It is not on the record subject to an oath. Both retainer letters are provided here to set up efficiently the adversarial process of litigating the standard of care in this case.

The attached materials collectively prepare you to simulate taking and defending depositions involving these respective experts. Depositions are the "bread and butter" of tort law lawyering. While this simulation involves expert witnesses, lawyers might also be conducting depositions of each doctor, the patient, and any witnesses with knowledge of the underlying facts.

II. SAM KENNEDY: CLIENT INTAKE MEMORANDUM

PLAINTIFF: Sam Kennedy
DOB: 7/9/1990
ADDRESS: 1119 Brookington Avenue
                    Palsgraf, Tortsylvania

Sam Kennedy is an eighth grade English teacher in the town of Palsgraf, Tortsylvania. One of Sam's back molars was causing discomfort. Sam wanted to get it taken care of over winter break so as to not miss any work. Sam scheduled an initial consultation with Dr. Ellington, a dental generalist in Sam's hometown, for December 8.

During the consultation/appointment, Dr. Ellington performed an examination, took x-rays, and determined that Sam needed a root canal in the bottom second molar on the right due to advanced decay. After the root canal procedure, Sam was given an ibuprofen prescription for pain.

While many dentists typically prescribe antibiotics as a precautionary measure, Dr. Ellington believes antibiotics are now being over-prescribed and is consequently hesitant to prescribe them without any medical indications.

Two weeks later, Sam's pain was not getting any better despite following all of Dr. Ellington's orders. Sam was now experiencing other troubling symptoms as well, such as swelling, fever, and nausea. Sam called Dr. Ellington's office and the receptionist said Sam should just report these symptoms at the scheduled follow-up appointment the next week.

Sam's symptoms worsened. When Sam's fever spiked to 102 degrees, Sam went to Palsgraf Emergency Room. Sam described the symptoms and recent dental work during hospital intake. The attending ER physician, Dr. Shay Robertson, ordered x-rays on Sam's jaw and a complete blood count (CBC) to determine the source of the fever. The x-rays revealed a metal object in the back molar where the root canal had been performed. The blood work revealed an elevated white blood count, suggesting an infection.

Sam was subsequently admitted for observation and kept for two days on a regimen of intravenous antibiotics, anti-inflammatories for the facial swelling, pain medication, and anti-nausea medication. Sam was under the care of Dr. Beth Morgan, M.D. throughout the hospitalization.

Upon discharge, Sam was prescribed additional antibiotics and pain medication, and was instructed to follow up with an endodontist as soon as possible. There is no specialist practicing in Sam's hometown. After the infection was fully treated, Sam was referred to Endodontist Rachel Salyer in the City of Clarksville, Tortsylvania over three and a half hours away. Salyer was the closest provider that took Sam's insurance and was taking new patients.

III. SAM KENNEDY: NEW CLIENT INTAKE FORM

TYPE OF CASE: Negligence—Medical Malpractice; Products Liability

STATUTE OF LIMITATIONS: 1 year

CLIENT NAME	Sam Kennedy
DOB	July 9, 1990
ADDRESS	1119 Brookington Avenue Palsgraf, Tortsylvania
PHONE NUMBER	(513) 499-5637
OCCUPATION INFORMATION	• 8th Grade English Teacher • Palsgraf Middle School, Palsgraf, Tortsylvania
DATE OF INJURY/ TIME FRAME	• 12/8 (initial visit) • Treatment: 12/8–1/3

POTENTIAL DEFENDANT 1	• Dr. Taylor Ellington, DMD
	• DOB: 11/20/1972
	• ADDRESS: Ellington Family Dentistry
	                    716 Smiles Way
	                    Palsgraf, Tortsylvania
	• OCCUPATION: General Dentistry. Sole practitioner.
	• SALARY: $185,000 a year (estimate)

POTENTIAL DEFENDANT 2	• Rotarious, Inc. (file manufacturer)
BRIEF DESCRIPTION	Dental injury after piece of dental file broke off in patient's mouth during a root canal procedure.
PROVIDERS TO SEND MEDICAL RECORDS AND BILLING REQUESTS	• Ellington Family Dentistry (Dr. Taylor Ellington) • Palsgraf Apothecary • Palsgraf Community Hospital • Clarksville Endodontics (Dr. Rachel Salyer)
SALARY/ WAGE LOSS IF APPLICABLE TIME MISSED	• $42,000/year • Wages lost: $875 per week • 2 weeks missed ($875 x2): $1,750.00
DAMAGES INFORMATION	• Past medical expenses • Future medical expenses? • Pain & Suffering • Lost Wages
STILL TREATING?	No

IV. AFFIDAVIT OF TREATING PHYSICIAN MORGAN

BEFORE ME, the undersigned authority personally appeared Beth Morgan, who being duly sworn deposes and says:

1. My name is Beth Morgan.

2. I am licensed by the State of Tortsylvania with full privileges to practice medicine within the State of Tortsylvania.

3. My practice is general surgery.

4. My private practice is located at 4567 Eagle Lane, in Palsgraf, Tortsylvania.

5. I have full privileges at Palsgraf Community Hospital and serve in an on-call rotation at this facility.

6. Dr. Shay Robertson was the attending physician when Sam Kennedy (hereinafter "Patient") was admitted to Palsgraf Community Hospital on December 23.

7. Patient was admitted with a high fever indicative of infection and swelling and pain in the jaw and mouth centered around the bottom right second molar.

8. X-rays performed in the Emergency Department revealed an unidentified piece of metal under the skin in this general area.

9. A complete blood count revealed Patient had an elevated white blood cell count, indicative of infection.

10. Patient was under my care during admission from December 23 through December 25.

11. I treated Patient with intravenous antibiotics for the infection and pain medication for the swelling and irritation throughout the duration of hospitalization.

12. Patient reported to me that the pain and infection began after a prior dental procedure.

13. Once the condition was under control, Patient was discharged with prescriptions for antibiotics and pain medication and instructed to follow up with an endodontist to address the underlying condition.

FURTHER AFFIANT SAYETH NAUGHT.

Dr. Beth Morgan, M.D.
Dr. Beth Morgan, M.D.
Print Name

STATE OF TORTSYLVANIA
COUNTY OF CLARK

Subscribed to and sworn before me by Beth Morgan on this 15th day of March.

Lashaunda Miller
NOTARY PUBLIC, STATE-AT-LARGE

MY COMMISSION EXPIRES: October 10, 2029

V. AFFIDAVIT OF TREATING PHYSICIAN SALYER

BEFORE ME, the undersigned authority personally appeared Rachel Salyer, who being duly sworn deposes and says:

1. My name is Rachel Salyer.

2. I am licensed by the State of Tortsylvania with full privileges to practice medicine within the State of Tortsylvania.

3. My practice specialty is endodontics, the treatment of tooth pain, dental pulp, and root canal treatments.

4. My office is located at 2789 Dogwood Lane, Suite 425, in Clarksville, Tortsylvania.

5. I am Sam Kennedy's (hereinafter "Patient") treating physician. I began treating Patient on December 27.

6. On December 27, I performed x-ray imaging on Patient and discovered a twisted file component that had been left inside the bottom right second molar.

7. I found this molar to be infected as evidenced by the swelling and irritation.

8. Patient returned to my office on December 28 for treatment and again on January 3 for a crown on this same tooth.

9. Patient reported that the symptoms began with a root canal procedure performed by another doctor on December 8.

10. Patient's symptoms are consistent with those likely to occur from a foreign object remaining in a surgical incision.

FURTHER AFFIANT SAYETH NAUGHT.

Dr. Rachel Salyer, M.D.
<u>**Dr. Rachel Salyer, M.D.**</u>
Print Name

STATE OF TORTSYLVANIA
COUNTY OF CLARK

Subscribed to and sworn before me by Beth Morgan on this 15th day of March.

Lashaunda Miller
NOTARY PUBLIC, STATE-AT-LARGE

MY COMMISSION EXPIRES: <u>October 10, 2029</u>

VI. STIPULATION OF FACTS

PALSGRAF CIRCUIT COURT
CASE NO. 19-CI-81956
Electronically Filed

SAM KENNEDY,   PLAINTIFF

v.

TAYLOR ELLINGTON, D.M.D.,   DEFENDANT

DEFENDANT TAYLOR ELLINGTON'S STIPULATION OF FACTS

The Defendant in this action stipulates to the following facts:

1. Dr. Taylor Ellington, D.M.D. is the solo general dentistry practitioner at Ellington Family Dentistry located at 716 Smiles Way, Palsgraf, Tortsylvania.

2. Dr. Ellington treated Sam Kennedy on December 8 for pain in the bottom right second molar.

3. Dr. Ellington performed an x-ray of the area and determined that a root canal was needed because the root had become infected through advanced decay.

4. Dr. Ellington anesthetized the area and then made an opening in the indicated tooth.

5. Dr. Ellington used a twisted file that had been used two previous times.

6. The twisted file was made of nickel titanium and disinfected before use.

7. Dr. Ellington used the twisted file to clean the infected area and remove the bad pulp.

8. The canal was then filled with a permanent material called Gutta percha and a cap was placed on top.

9. Dr. Ellington wrote Kennedy a prescription for twenty-four (24) Ibuprofen 800mg with directions to take one (1) every four (4) to six (6) hours as needed for pain.

VII. PLAINTIFF'S EXPERT RETAINER AGREEMENT

Dr. Pangri Kim, D.D.S.

March 22

Plaintiff's Law Firm
827 Calicat Road
Palsgraf, Tortsylvania

     RE: Sam Kennedy

To Whom It May Concern:

     At your request, I have reviewed records on dental treatment provided to Sam Kennedy by Dr. Taylor Ellington, D.M.D., of Ellington Family Dentistry and Dr. Rachel Salyer, D.D.S, of Clarksville Endodontics. I am licensed to practice Dentistry in the states of Tortsylvania, California, and New York, and have been licensed since 1996. I have written textbooks in the field of general dentistry and endodontics. I have taught numerous specialized courses focused specifically on root canals. My primary practice is located in San Francisco, California. I am considered one of the leading national experts in the field of endodontics.

     I have completed over a thousand root canals and I am familiar with the standards for a reasonably prudent dentist in root canal procedures and patient care. I am familiar with the standards for communications with the patient regarding the root canal procedure, complications therefrom, and any subsequent treatment. I am familiar with the standards governing treatment after an unsuccessful procedure and the proper course of action following dental equipment breakage.

     All of the opinions set forth herein are expressed to a reasonable medical probability. In reaching this conclusion, I relied on the following definitions of negligence, ordinary care, and proximate cause:

     "Negligence" with reference to the conduct of Dr. Taylor Ellington, D.M.D. means the failure to use ordinary care, meaning the failure to do that which a dentist of ordinary or reasonable prudence would have done under the same or similar circumstance or doing that which a dentist of ordinary or reasonable prudence would not have done under the same or similar circumstances.

     "Ordinary Care" with reference to the conduct of Dr. Taylor Ellington, D.M.D. means the degree of care that a dentist of ordinary or reasonable prudence would use under the same or similar circumstances.

     "Proximate Cause" with reference to the conduct of Dr. Taylor Ellington, D.M.D means that which in a natural and continuous sequence, produced an event, and without cause such an event would not have occurred; and in order to be a proximate cause, the act or omission complained of must be such that a physician exercising ordinary care would have foreseen that the event, or some similar event, might reasonably result therefrom. There may be more than one proximate cause of an event.

The summary that follows, and my opinions expressed herein, are based on my review of the records from Dr. Ellington, Dr. Morgan of Palsgraf Community Hospital, and Dr. Salyer. I have relied upon Sam's statement that Dr. Ellington never informed Sam that the file remained in the tooth after the root canal and that Dr. Ellington made no subsequent efforts to determine the source of the continuing pain and swelling.

During Sam's December 8 visit, Dr. Ellington performed a root canal on the bottom right second molar. During this root canal procedure, a twisted dental file broke off in Sam's root and remained there after the root canal as reflected by the subsequent x-rays performed at Palsgraf Community Hospital and Dr. Salyer's office.

A reasonably prudent dentist should always inspect the equipment for any breakage or other failure, review x-rays taken during the consultation, during the procedure, and following the procedure, and promptly notify the patient of any suspected issues. The misuse of files beyond their intended use as specified by the manufacturer is not an acceptable medical practice. All equipment must be thoroughly inspected before and after any and all dental procedures. The standard of care requires that all dentistry practices have policies and procedures in place to inspect the equipment before and after use for any anomalies or defects.

Files do occasionally break off during a root canal. Presence of the file inside the tooth can cause significant pain and discomfort for the patient. The standard of care requires that the dentist make a reasonable effort to extract the broken piece. Failing to accomplish this, the standard of care requires the dentist to note the breakage in the patient's chart, inform the patient of the breakage, and closely monitor the patient over the course of future visits for any clinical symptoms of infection or other problems. To this end, the standard of care also requires that dentist always investigate the cause of the patient's pain, beginning with an x-ray of the indicated area. Although a dentist should work to immediately remove the instrument, complicated root canal cases should be referred to endodontists as this is the accepted national standard of care.

Dr. Ellington did not review the requisite x-rays or promptly inform Sam of any defects of the instrument following the root canal. It is my opinion that this failure to inspect the instruments, perform/examine x-rays, and investigate the patient's complaints of pain following the root canal fell below the standard of care. It is my opinion to a reasonable degree of medical certainty that these failures in the standard of care caused the patient a dangerous infection and caused pain and swelling in the face, which likely caused admission to Palsgraf Community Hospital. The cause of Sam Kennedy's continued pain was likely the file, which had been left in the tooth. This is borne out by, among other things, the fact that the pain ceased once Dr. Salyer removed the file.

I will make myself available for deposition and I will prepare an expert report consistent with this retainer agreement. Please be in touch with my office once you have finalized these dates so that I can make travel arrangements and clear my calendar.

Sincerely,

Dr. Pangri Kim

Dr. Pangri Kim, D.D.S.

VIII. DEFENDANT'S EXPERT RETAINER AGREEMENT

Dr. Devon Johnson, D.D.S.

March 30

Defendant's Law Firm
17736 Cardinal Lane
Palsgraf, Tortsylvania

RE: Dr. Taylor Ellington, D.M.D.

To Whom It May Concern:

Per your request, I have reviewed the medical records detailing the dental treatment provided by Dr. Taylor Ellington, D.M.D. to patient Sam Kennedy. I have been licensed in Tortsylvania since 2001. I have performed hundreds of root canals in Tortsylvania throughout my career and I am familiar with the standard of care for a reasonably prudent dentist here.

From my review of the relevant records, it is my opinion to a reasonable degree of medical certainty that Dr. Ellington's care did not fall below an acceptable standard of care in the treatment of patient Sam Kennedy.

Root canals are not all alike. Some may be very complicated. Infections can arise for multiple reasons. Consequently, Sam Kennedy's infection could have been caused by a multitude of things, such as prior injuries, failure to follow after-care instructions, or adverse health indications. Similarly, it is not uncommon for general dentists to perform root canals nor is it unacceptable to reuse dental files. Dr. Ellington's use would be no different.

Although failing to review patient x-rays systemically is not consistent with the general standard of care, there can be exceptions during uniquely busy periods and office disruptions. I can say to a reasonable degree of certainty that it is not uncommon for dentists to occasionally omit screening x-rays while managing a solo practice comprehensively. The facts would have to be understood in context. General dentistry practices in this community often see a high number of patients in any given day with a range of potential problems. This fact does not necessarily prove that a practitioner breached a standard of care. It is simply the reality of busy practice demands.

In my opinion to a reasonable degree of medical probability, based on my education, training, and experience, Dr. Ellington did not breach the standard of care expected of a general dentist solo practitioner. I will testify under oath to the same if necessary.

Please contact my office if you have any questions. I will prepare the expert report before the due date we discussed.

Sincerely,

Dr. Devon Johnson

Dr. Devon Johnson, D.D.S.

IX. DEPOSITION PRACTICE GUIDELINES

Tortsylvania Tort Law Magazine

Preparing for Your First Deposition
By: Julianne Tackett, J.D.

The importance of depositions is often overlooked in traditional tort law studies. The true value and significance of depositions in tort litigation, however, cannot be overstated. Depositions help lawyers focus on the key issues in the case and gain insights to what the other side's strategy might be. Depositions can determine if a case settles before trial, potentially saving hundreds of thousands of dollars. Depositions help lawyers determine which witnesses will be relatable to a local jury if the case proceeds to trial. You may have an expert who—on paper—seems perfect for your case, only then to discover during a deposition that the expert does not make a good witness due to nerves, demeanor, disposition, etc.

The standard practice in prepping a client or witness for a deposition is a preparation meeting in the lawyer's office going over the general format of a deposition and practicing anticipated questions. It is vital that the witness understand the deposition process in order to best pursue or defend the case. A preparation meeting might include the following advice:

- Be honest always.

- You will be under oath and there will be a court reporter typing everything you say. You must give verbal answers. Do not simply shake your head yes or no.

- Wait until the entire question is asked before answering. Do not speak over anyone because the court reporter must document everything that every person involved says. That's difficult to do when more than one person is speaking at a time.

- Take the time that you need to compose your answers before you begin speaking.

- Only answer the question that was asked and nothing more. For example, consider being asked "have you had lunch today?" and responding with "yes, I ate pizza." This answer did not respond to only the question asked. The question was whether you had eaten lunch, not what you ate. This simple example helps clients understand the importance of listening and responding to only what is asked.

- You can always ask for a break. It is better to gather yourself for a few moments than to say something that could potentially damage your case.

- If your attorney starts to speak, like saying "objection," do not answer opposing counsel's question until your own attorney directs you to answer. Giving your attorney a chance to object is another reason to take a moment before responding.

- Body language and facial expressions are important to consider. If a party comes across as aloof, dishonest, or disinterested, opposing counsel might become more comfortable letting the case get to a jury. Conversely, if a party comes across as sincere, honest, and relatable, opposing counsel might be more inclined to settle than to roll the dice with a jury.

Depositions are a critical part of tort lawyering. They allow the facts to solidify and lawyering strategies to take shape. Learning to take depositions early in your career will help you master substantive tort law as well.

This article gives just a quick preview for new lawyers. Consider reading sample transcripts of depositions or watching sample videos to prepare for your first deposition. There are endless practice materials available to prepare you for this exciting first lawyering experience!

X. THE SIMULATION EXERCISE

Lawyering depositions is a valuable skill to practice early in your career. Sam Kennedy's case will likely rise or fall on whether Sam can prove that the dentist breached a governing standard of care in the community. This simulation exercise positions students to defend and take depositions from competing experts in the case. Securing strong testimony at the discovery phase of the case is critical. In this "battle of the experts," one expert argues that the dentist did breach standards of care causing Sam's harms. A competing expert argues that the dentist-defendant's conduct was within the standard of care and did not cause Sam's harms.

Note the relative qualifications and the respective locations of each expert's dental practice. Consider why tort law might regularly yield geographic differences like this. Consider how the selection of a particular expert might be used strategically in deposition or trial to strengthen your respective case.

Depositions are a lawyer's first chance to secure the testimony of experts under oath. Lawyers seek to elicit the conclusions outlined in the respective retainer letters and expert reports. Depositions use a question and response approach to extract the conclusions. Depositions might also be a critical tool to facilitate settlement as the facts solidify. Depositions are costly though and they involve extensive preparation of testifying witnesses.

Depositions do not take place in front of a judge. They are governed by procedural and evidentiary rules though. Attorneys work with a court reporter to record the proceeding and preserve objections on the record.

Your professor will provide further instruction on the exact structure of this deposition assignment. You will likely be divided into four teams to execute this simulation. The first two groups will simulate the deposition of the plaintiff's expert only. Group 1 will represent the plaintiff's expert witness in preparing the expert for a deposition and primarily questioning the witness. Group 2 will represent the defendant while questioning the plaintiff's expert witness. The second two groups will simulate the deposition of the defendant's expert only. Group 3 will represent the defendant's expert witness in preparing the witness for a deposition and primarily questioning the witness. Group 4 will represent the plaintiff while questioning the defendant's expert witness. These are parallel exercises. Alternatively, the class could be divided in half and the same process completed twice by deposing and cross-examining plaintiff's expert and then deposing and questioning defendant's expert.

For those students taking a deposition proactively for your client, you might first simulate a meeting preparing the client for what to expect in the deposition. What would you tell your client? How should they answer questions? The examining counsel's purpose is to compile admissible evidence and to lock in the testimony of the witness. Students taking a deposition for their own client should consider starting broad and working to narrow. You should have an outline of questions to extract the key conclusions in question and answer format. While ordinarily considerable time would be spent in the deposition on the qualifications and credentials of the witness, students will give short attention to this task to focus on applying standard of care concepts.

For those challenging an expert witness, opposing counsel will work to draw out the weaknesses and critiques of the stated positions. What questions reveal weaknesses effectively? Remember the plaintiff's counsel holds the burden of proof and has to prove by a preponderance of the evidence that the breach in the standard of care more likely than not caused the plaintiff's harm.

Your professor will provide specific instructions for the deposition simulation. You will likely be given time to prepare and strategize your questioning and then time to perform the simulation.

Have fun with this exercise. Depositions are not a lawyering skill that gets depicted often in courtroom dramas and films, but it is a skill that makes, breaks, and shapes a case in the real world.

CHAPTER 3

NEGLIGENCE: CAUSATION

I. INTRODUCTION

Causation is an exciting and sophisticated area of tort law to study. It can be helpful to think of causation as the bridge between breaches in the standard of care and the damages incurred. Does the one flow to the other? Causation asks whether the breach was the actual source of the harm and whether the defendant should have to pay for the harms that occurred even if it was the source of the harm. Causation is a two-step inquiry.

The first step is an exercise in counterfactuals. Factual causation analysis works like the deleted scenes bonus content in a movie DVD. Imagine you could rewrite a scene in which the defendant never breached the standard of care. Then you fast-forward ahead to see if, once the breach is removed, does this removal eliminate the harms that the plaintiff suffered? If the plaintiff is nonetheless injured, then the defendant's breach is not the factual cause of the plaintiff's harms.

In many cases though there are multiple explanations for the plaintiff's harms. For example, what if two tortious acts collectively combine to create one harm, such as when one speeding driver hits a jaywalking pedestrian, each combining to injure a passenger in the car. Your casebook has presented a string of cases introducing you to these more complex factual causation scenarios. In sum, as long as the defendant's conduct is at least "a substantial factor," the plaintiff can prove factual causation. While this rule is a bit indeterminate, remember that causation issues are jury questions. In close cases, focus less on getting the "answer" and more on framing competing arguments for the plaintiff and the defendant to respectively make their factual causation case to the jury.

The proximate cause question is next. Think about proximate cause like first putting on binoculars and then separately looking in your rearview mirror. Proximate cause looks to the foreseeability of the harms that the plaintiff suffered. Think about this inquiry like you are standing with a set of binoculars surveying the landscape coming up ahead after your breach. At the moment of the breach, was it within the tortfeasor's view that the breach could cause the harms that the plaintiff suffered? This inquiry rules out harms that are too remote to be foreseeable.

Proximate cause can also involve separately looking in the rearview mirror from the harms that the plaintiff did suffer back to the moment of the breach. The purpose of this backward-looking inquiry is to look for any other factors or actors that may have intervened so as to supersede the defendant's liability. This inquiry rules out any unforeseeable interventions between breach and injury that might cut off the chain of liability.

The proximate cause inquiry is heavily policy based. There may be injuries for which it is factually possible to trace the injuries back to the defendant's breach in the standard of care, but for which the community might prefer not to hold the defendant liable as a policy matter. For example, consider an outbreak of a contagious virus like COVID-19. What if we conclude that a nursing home was negligent in allowing the virus to spread from patient 0 to patients 1, 2, and 3. Then patients 1, 2, and 3—before knowing they were contagious—spread the disease further to patients 4, 5, and 6. The nursing home might be factually linked to the infection of patients 1–6, but as a policy matter, is that the outcome that we elect as a society?

Communities might instead worry that over-punishing the nursing home will drive up long-term care costs for everyone. The answer to whether liability should be imposed for the harms suffered by patients 1–6 sits in the local community's assessment of the social, political, and economic implications of doing so. For example, consider how social attitudes change across communities and over time towards acts like vaping, second-hand smoke exposure, childhood vaccinations, drunk driving, and texting and driving. There is lots of room for effective persuasive advocacy when presenting proximate cause issues to a jury.

This simulation revisits the Sam Kennedy case file. It considers how causation arguments might develop. We first met Sam Kennedy in Chapter 2. We initially received some intake files in the case, but we had not yet conducted discovery to learn other facts that might complicate the case. In this chapter, defense counsel has received some new facts in the discovery process and through outside research.

Discovery is the process of uncovering facts about the case. As you will learn in your civil procedure course, lawyers can ask for information through many discovery tools like depositions, interrogatories (written questions) and requests for production of documents. These discovery tools help a lawyer prepare the case and prove the facts that were mere allegations at the outset of the lawsuit. The following materials reveal excerpted results of pre-trial discovery that complicate causation.

In the preceding standard of care chapter, you practiced taking and defending expert depositions. This chapter challenges you to prepare to depose the plaintiff, Sam Kennedy, on issues of causation. The instructions and materials that follow guide you through preparing a causation litigation strategy based on these new facts.

II. DISCOVERY DOCUMENT PRODUCTION

In the discovery phase of Sam Kennedy's case, defense counsel raised this document request:

> *Request for Production 18:* Produce any documents relating to any injuries of any nature that the Plaintiff suffered to the mouth or face in the preceding two years, such as, but not limited to, police reports, medical reports, insurance claims, worker's compensation filings, and civil claims.

This request yielded production of a police report. It revealed an injury that occurred after the medical procedure that Dr. Ellington performed and before hospitalization. No further information was produced. Your upcoming deposition of Sam will present a chance to inquire further about these facts and their relevance to causation.

POLICE REPORT

Palsgraf County Sheriff's Office						Report No. 83749929	
Offender				*Height*	*Eyes*	*Hair*	
Cameron	Roe	Riley		5'09	Brown	Brown	
Address			*City*	*State*			
249 Tarasoff Court			Palsgraf	Tortsylvania			
Date				*Reporting Officer*		*Badge No.*	
12/15				Det. Meyer		48776	

Summary of Incident

On the night of 12/14, police were called by neighbors of victim, Sam Taylor Kennedy, regarding a domestic argument that could be heard next door. A neighbor reported to 911 that she could hear Cameron shouting at Sam and a physical scuffle of some sort.

Upon arrival, Detective Meyer knocked on the door. Sam Kennedy answered. Det. Meyer noticed discoloration on the right side of Sam Kennedy's jaw. Sam Kennedy revealed that Cameron Riley caused the injury following an argument. Sam said that the incident was resolved and required no police intervention.

Det. Meyer then followed standard protocol for a first-time domestic violence incident. As this was the first incident on record for Cameron Riley and because Sam Kennedy had strongly elected not to press charges, this report serves as documentation that the incident occurred.

III. WEBSITE EXCERPT

Your research as defense counsel reveals the following text excerpted from the Rotarious, Inc. website. This is a website selling dental products to consumers (dental practices) directly.

This rotary file is used in dentistry practices for a variety of purposes. This model is a nickel titanium file used to expose the glide path during a root canal. This state-of-the-art design is perfect for clearing the root canal and determining the working length with extreme precision and efficiency. This model is designed for single use and comes sterile, so there is no need for reprocessing. This file should only be used by a licensed dentist or endodontist.

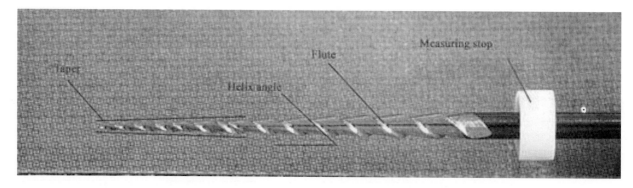

Model R-2000

IV. ONLINE PRODUCT REVIEWS

Your independent research as defense counsel further reveals the following online product reviews of the Model R-2000. These customer reviews suggest that this product might break more easily in dental procedures than comparable models. You will revisit and expand these facts further in Chapter 8 on Products Liability. For now, think about how these reviews complicate and challenge causation in Sam Kennedy's claim against the doctor.

MODEL R-2000, MANUFACTURED BY ROTARIOUS, INC.

July 3 ★

This feels like it's going to break when even the slightest pressure is applied. I don't like the feel of it. Sorry, not good enough for my dental practice.

January 29 ★★

We used one of these files only 4 times and it broke off in the patient's tooth canal. Cheap garbage.

February 1 ★★★★

I got about 6 uses out of these files, not just single use. Better than the last brand I bought.

March 31 ★

Very bad. Flimsy and thin. Do not buy.

April 9 ★★★★

Great product. Light and user-friendly.

May 7 ★★★

Works great as a single use but wouldn't recommend attempting multiple uses.

August 15 ★★★

Worked well.

August 17 ★★★

Worked great. Feels a little weak, but it's so affordable.

V. MODEL CAUSATION JURY INSTRUCTIONS

Your research finds the following model jury instructions that your judge in Tortsylvania often uses in negligence cases (relying on New Jersey model jury instructions). Remember that learning causation is hard for first-year law students, so it has to likewise be challenging for judges to explain these concepts to a lay jury. Jury instructions accordingly can be a great learning tool for new lawyers because they break down complex concepts into manageable steps.

Below are the jury instructions that the judge in Sam Kennedy's case might give to a jury should your case get to a jury. Here, the court is using "proximate cause" as an inclusive umbrella term for *both* factual causation and proximate causation. The court's language relating to "concurrent causes" aligns with your study of actual cause or factual causation. The language regarding the foreseeability of the harms aligns with your study of proximate cause. Use these jury instructions as a review tool to help you master causation concepts.

PROXIMATE CAUSE—WHERE THERE IS CLAIM THAT CONCURRENT CAUSES OF HARM ARE PRESENT AND CLAIM THAT SPECIFIC HARM WAS **NOT** FORESEEABLE (Approved 5/98)

NOTE TO JUDGE

This instruction is ... is designed to apply to appropriate negligence cases ... * * * To find proximate cause, you must first find that *[name of defendant or party]*'s negligence was a cause of the accident/incident/event. If you find that *[name of defendant or other party]*'s negligence is not a cause of the accident/incident/event, then you must find no proximate cause.

Second, you must find that *[name of defendant or other party]* negligence was a substantial factor that singly, or in combination with other causes, brought about the injury/loss/harm claimed by *[name of plaintiff]*. By substantial, it is meant that it was not a remote, trivial or inconsequential cause. The mere circumstance that there may also be another cause of the injury/loss/harm does not mean that there cannot be a finding of proximate cause. Nor is it necessary for the negligence of *[name of the defendant or other party]* to be the sole cause of *[name of plaintiff]*'s injury/loss/harm. However, you must find that *[name of defendant or other party]*'s negligence was a substantial factor in bringing about the injury/loss/harm.

Third, you must find that some injury/loss/harm to *[name of plaintiff]* must have been foreseeable. For the injury/loss/harm to be foreseeable, it is not necessary that the precise injury/loss/harm that occurred here was foreseeable by *[name of defendant or other party]*. Rather, a reasonable person should have anticipated the risk that *[name of defendant or other party]*'s conduct *[omission]* could cause some injury/loss/harm suffered by *[name of plaintiff]*. In other words, if some injury/loss/harm from *[name of defendant or other party]*'s negligence was within the realm of reasonable foreseeability, then the injury/loss/harm is considered foreseeable. On the other hand, if the risk of injury/loss/harm was so remote as not to be in the realm of reasonable foreseeability, you must find no proximate cause.

In sum, in order to find proximate cause, you must find that the negligence of *[name of defendant or other party]* was a substantial factor in bringing about the injury/loss/harm that occurred and that some harm to *[name of plaintiff]* was foreseeable from *[name of defendant or other party]*'s negligence.

VI. THE SIMULATION EXERCISE

For this causation simulation, you are defending Dr. Ellington in the dental malpractice suit introduced in the preceding chapter. You should assume for this chapter that Sam has sued both Dr. Ellington and the product manufacturer of the dental file.

Your supervising attorney asked you to review the partial discovery results and the research findings above. Your supervisor asked you to prepare a list of questions on just the causation elements. These are questions that your legal team will ask in Sam Kennedy's upcoming deposition based on these new facts. Your goal is to prepare Dr. Ellington's legal team to complicate and challenge the plaintiff's ability to prove causation.

Your supervisor worries privately that a jury may find that Dr. Ellington breached standards of care. The current working defense strategy focuses on minimizing the damages and raising causation defenses. Your supervisor believes that Kennedy's deposition has the potential to lead the plaintiff to a reasonable settlement if defense counsel can elicit testimony that the infection and subsequent medical care were attributable to other causes.

As you prepare an outline of questions to direct the deposition questioning of Sam Kennedy, consider carefully whether the facts raise factual or proximate causation issues. As a useful starting point, think about the timing. Events that occurred after Dr. Ellington's care likely raise proximate cause issues. Events that occurred concurrent with Dr. Ellington's care likely raise factual causation issues.

Think carefully about how to elicit evidence in a question and answer format. You cannot just jump to the finale and ask penultimate questions like, "isn't it true that your injuries were actually caused by an incident of domestic violence on December 14?" The witness is not qualified to make such conclusions and the witness is adversarial. Rather, you have to build slowly to that implication by asking about the relevant dates, the injury locations, etc.

Depositions are central to building negligence cases for trial. Taking and defending depositions are essential "bread and butter" skills that lawyers develop throughout their practice. This simulation brings causation issues to life by preparing for a critical deposition in the Sam Kennedy case.

CHAPTER 4

NEGLIGENCE: DUTY OF CARE

I. INTRODUCTION

Duty of care analysis integrates law and policy in tort law. The negligence elements that you studied in Chapters 2 and 3 are rooted in more fact-specific inquiries that are directed to juries for resolution. Whether the defendant owed a duty of care to the plaintiff, however, is a question of law for the judge. This procedural point is important because a case may never get to a jury if the plaintiff cannot satisfy this element. Duty of care issues can lead to an early case dismissal at the motion stage.

Sequentially, negligence elements are ordered as (1) duty, (2) breach, (3) causation, and (4) damages. This list of elements presents duty first. Often, however, the duty of care content is presented later in the course material after students have already studied standards of care and causation, as this simulation book does. For lawyering purposes though, duty of care issues hold high threshold importance because they may defeat the claim as a matter of law.

The historic roots of the duty of care analysis were far more restrictive and nuanced for plaintiffs to overcome. Privity concepts might have limited the ability of a consumer, for example, to sue a product manufacturer if the plaintiff was not the direct purchaser and thus not in privity with the manufacturer. These concepts have less modern relevance but are very helpful to understanding modern rules of products liability and duty of care.

If you have already studied causation, it is helpful to reflect on what you already know about the duty of care element before you proceed. The duty of care issue also likely came up in your course in the famous dialogue between Justices Cardozo and Andrews in the *Palsgraf* opinions. Justice Cardozo held that the Long Island Railroad owed no duty to Ms. Palsgraf and thus her claim could not proceed as a matter of law. A jury never heard from Ms. Palsgraf at all. Justice Andrews, in dissent, would have pushed the liability question to the jury as one of foreseeability within the proximate cause element of negligence. The difference the iconic judicial dispute made sat heavily in the question of "who." Would the judge or the jury decide the outcome? Both judges seemed to agree that the case was weak for Ms. Palsgraf.

Modern tort law imposes a sweeping duty on defendants to act reasonably. That broad rule covers most of the cases that you will study and litigate. In the standards of care cases that you studied in your casebook, for example, you saw relationships (e.g., doctor-patient, lawyer-client, landlord-tenant) creating duties of care. You also saw acts, such as driving, flying, and repairing creating duties of care. The duty of care element is easily established by our acts and our relationships in most cases. The duty of care material that you study in class is thus primarily focused on the narrow exceptions and even narrower exceptions to the exceptions of these general rules. It is important to not lose sight of this sweeping general rule structure as you explore these narrow rule exceptions.

Your casebook chapter on duty of care likely focused on special rules governing the duty of care element. These special duty of care issues are heavily policy-based and thus subject to great persuasive advocacy. One unifying lens to study this material is through the lens of bright-line rules versus indeterminate outcomes. In some of the rules that you studied in this unit, like the economic loss rule, negligent infliction of emotional distress, and duties to unborn children, the rules will lead to harsh outcomes, but predictable ones.

It is important to consider the challenges of client counseling here. Imagine advising a fiancée that witnessing first-hand the tragic harms suffered by their loved one is not recoverable in tort because the two do not share a qualifying relationship to trigger liability. Bright-line rules provide certainty and predictability, but they also lead to harsh outcomes.

On the other hand, you will also study murkier rules that provide less predictability. Consider, for example, trying to advise a school district, parent, spouse, or teacher on the duties of care to which these entities and individuals will be held if they suspect someone they know might engage in an act of violence. Do they have a duty to report? To protect? To intervene? We see headlines monthly revealing the challenges of these questions. The legal system will necessarily provide an answer retroactively, but the legal uncertainty makes it hard for professionals and loved ones to function contemporaneously in these decisive moments.

This unit also considers rules that very narrowly carve out exceptions to the sweeping general rules, such as pure economic loss, emotional distress, and unborn children. For these units, consider the policy implications. Why would the law opt for a narrower rule than ordinary negligence principles would suggest? Generally speaking, it is because the ordinary rules risk unrestrained liability or present challenging litigation issues. The trade-off yields a bright-line rule, but bright-line rules bring harsh results.

This simulation assignment considers these questions of uncertainty and indeterminacy in a lawyering context. This simulation returns to the Sharp Shooter's fact pattern introduced in Chapter 1. You will consider whether a spouse is liable for sending a text to her husband knowing that he was prone to violent outbursts directed at her and knowing that he was at a shooting range when she sent it. It asks you to make persuasive arguments in a motion for summary judgment (judgment as a matter of law). You will develop complex arguments that put together substantive rules, procedural standards, facts, and policy considerations.

The attached materials provide the text that the wife sent, an affidavit that the wife signed, and a binding case governing in our jurisdiction.

―――――――――

II. WIFE'S TEXT

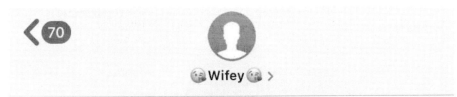

> I know you R @ the range. Sorry to do this by text, I knew you would lose it when I told you. I'm divorcing U. 😔

III. WIFE'S AFFIDAVIT

Wendy Wife gave the following sworn statement to investigators regarding her text message and her decision to leave Harold.

VOLUNTARY STATEMENT	
Wendy Wife	*Redacted*
Name	Social Security Number
Unemployed	n/a
Place of Work	Role
6345 Matrimony Blvd. Palsgraf, Tortsylvania 12345	
Address	

I, <u>Wendy Wife</u>, hereby make the following statement:

I finally decided to leave my husband because I couldn't deal with his temper anymore. Every minor inconvenience would cause him to blow up and throw a temper tantrum. He screams and yells and sometimes he will even break things. I tried everything to get Harold to control his anger. When I threatened to leave him last year, I only decided to stay if he agreed to go to anger management classes. But the classes didn't seem to help. It's gotten so bad lately that I've been afraid to disagree with him in fear of sending him into one of his tantrums. I wanted to wait until he was out of the house to tell him the news to avoid witnessing his anger. I knew that the morning of March 4 would be a good time to tell him because he would be gone for several hours at the range. I knew he could blow off steam there when he learned the news. Harold left the house around 10:30 a.m., so I packed up my things, loaded the car, and texted him that I was leaving him. I was on the road, headed towards my freedom by 11:15. I feel truly sick about what happened at the range, but Harold is solely responsible for his conduct. I am a victim just as much as those who were injured by his shooting. I have to live knowing who my husband was.

I swear (or affirm) that the information in the statement above is true to the best of my knowledge or belief.

Wendy Wife	March 9	9 a.m.
(Witness' Signature)	(Date)	Time

Sworn to and subscribed before me on this date.

Clayton Brown	March 9	9 a.m.
(Investigator's Signature)	(Date)	Time

IV. LEGAL RESEARCH

(A) PROCEDURAL RULES

In Chapter 1 you drafted a complaint alleging intentional tort claims against Harold. After the initial case pleadings, the case moves to discovery. You will learn more about the discovery process in your civil procedure course. It is a phase of the case that sits after the complaint and before pre-trial motions and trial.

Discovery disclosed the two new documents presented in the preceding materials. These documents reveal that the parties both agree on the underlying facts. The wife sent the text seeking divorce. She knew that Harold had anger management issues. She knew that he would be upset by the text. She knew he was at the gun range.

The parties disagree though on whether a duty of care arises from these facts. A motion for summary judgment is a procedural maneuver that either party can deploy when the parties agree on the facts and only need a judge's legal conclusion. Your procedural legal research reveals the following standard for granting summary judgment motions.

This is a federal rule that would apply in federal court. In civil procedure you will study whether a lawsuit should be filed in federal or state court. Many tort law cases will be state cases applying state rules of procedure. The federal rules are used for this simulation because it likely reinforces your civil procedure course content.

(a) MOTION FOR SUMMARY JUDGMENT OR PARTIAL SUMMARY JUDGMENT.

The court shall grant summary judgment if the movant shows that there is no genuine dispute as to any material fact and the movant is entitled to judgment as a matter of law. The court should state on the record the reasons for granting or denying the motion.

(B) SUBSTANTIVE LAW

Your substantive legal research further reveals that the state of Tortsylvania has adopted the reasoning and holding of this excerpted New Jersey case on the duties of care owed when texting a recipient who is driving. *Kubert v. Best* considers an appeal of a motion for summary judgment dismissing the negligence claim. This case excerpt is procedurally, substantively, and factually relevant to your assignment.

It also powerfully reveals themes introduced in Chapters 2 and 3 about the transformative role of depositions and discovery. *Kubert v. Best* reveals that the driver gave one set of facts at the scene of the accident. Through discovery, the facts changed considerably as documents and depositions challenged the truthfulness of earlier statements.

Kubert v. Best

432 N.J. Super. 495
2013

Opinion

* * * Plaintiffs Linda and David Kubert were grievously injured by an eighteen-year-old driver who was texting while driving and crossed the center-line of the road. Their claims for compensation from the young driver have been settled and are no longer part of this lawsuit. Plaintiffs appeal the trial court's dismissal of their claims against the driver's seventeen-year-old friend who was texting the driver much of the day and sent a text message to him immediately before the accident.

New Jersey prohibits texting while driving. A statute under our motor vehicle laws makes it illegal to use a cell phone that is not "hands-free" while driving, except in certain specifically-described emergency situations. *N.J.S.A.* 39:4–97.3. An offender is subject to a fine of $100. *N.J.S.A.* 39:4–97.3(d). For future cases like this one, the State Legislature enacted a law, called the "Kulesh, Kubert, and Bolis Law," to provide criminal penalties for those who are distracted by use of a cell phone while driving and injure others. The new law explicitly permits a jury to infer that a driver who was using a hand-held cell phone and caused injury in an accident may be guilty of assault by auto, a fourth-degree crime if someone was injured seriously, thus exposing the driver to a potential sentence in state prison.

The issue before us is not directly addressed by these statutes or any case law that has been brought to our attention. We must determine as a matter of civil common law whether one who is texting from a location remote from the driver of a motor vehicle can be liable to persons injured because the driver was distracted by the text. We hold that the sender of a text message can potentially be liable if an accident is caused by texting, but only if the sender knew or had special reason to know that the recipient would view the text while driving and thus be distracted.

In this appeal, we must also decide whether plaintiffs have shown sufficient evidence to defeat summary judgment in favor of the remote texter. We conclude they have not. We affirm the trial court's order dismissing plaintiffs' complaint against the sender of the text messages, but we do not adopt the trial court's reasoning that a remote texter does not have a legal duty to avoid sending text messages to one who is driving.

I.

The Kuberts' claims against defendant Shannon Colonna, the teenage sender of the texts, were never heard by a jury. Since this appeal comes to us from summary judgment in favor of Colonna, we view all the evidence and reasonable inferences that can be drawn from the evidence favorably to plaintiffs, the Kuberts.

On the afternoon of September 21, 2009, David Kubert was riding his motorcycle, with his wife, Linda Kubert, riding as a passenger. As they came south around a curve on Hurd Street in Mine Hill Township, a pick-up truck being driven north by eighteen-year-old Kyle Best crossed the double center line of the roadway into their lane of travel. David Kubert attempted to evade the pick-up truck but could not. The front driver's side of the truck struck the Kuberts and their motorcycle. The collision severed, or nearly severed, David's left leg. It shattered Linda's left leg, leaving her fractured thighbone protruding out of the skin as she lay injured in the road.

Best stopped his truck, saw the severity of the injuries, and called 911. The time of the 911 call was 17:49:15, that is, fifteen seconds after 5:49 p.m. Best, a volunteer fireman, aided the Kuberts to the best of his ability until the police and emergency medical responders arrived. Medical treatment could not save either victim's leg. Both lost their left legs as a result of the accident.

After the Kuberts filed this lawsuit, their attorney developed evidence to prove Best's activities on the day of the accident. In September 2009, Best and Colonna were seeing each other socially but not exclusively; they were not boyfriend and girlfriend. Nevertheless, they texted each other many times each day. Best's cell phone record showed that he and Colonna texted each other sixty-two times on the day of the accident, about an equal number of texts originating from each. They averaged almost fourteen texts per hour for the four-and-a-half-hour, non-consecutive time-span they were in telephone contact on the day of the accident.

The telephone record also showed that, in a period of less than twelve hours on that day, Best had sent or received 180 text messages. In her deposition, Colonna acknowledged that it was her habit also to text more than 100 times per day. She said: "I'm a young teenager. That's what we do." She also testified that she generally did not pay attention to whether the recipient of her texts was driving a car at the time or not. She thought it was "weird" that plaintiffs' attorney was trying to pin her down on whether she knew that Best was driving when she texted him.

During the day of the accident, a Monday, Best and Colonna exchanged many text messages in the morning, had lunch together at his house, and watched television until he had to go to his part-time job at a YMCA in Randolph Township. The time record from the YMCA showed that Best punched in on a time clock at 3:35 p.m. At 3:49 p.m., Colonna texted him, but he did not respond at that time. He punched out of work at 5:41. A minute later, at 5:42, Best sent a text to Colonna. He then exchanged three text messages with his father, testifying at his deposition that he did so while in the parking lot of the YMCA and that the purpose was to notify his parents he was coming home to eat dinner with them.

The accident occurred about four or five minutes after Best began driving home from the YMCA. At his deposition, Best testified that he did not text while driving—meaning that it was not his habit to text when he was driving. He testified falsely at first that he did not text when he began his drive home from the YMCA on the day of the accident. But he was soon confronted with the telephone records, which he had seen earlier, and then he admitted that he and Colonna exchanged text messages within minutes of his beginning to drive.

The sequence of texts between Best and Colonna in the minutes before and after the accident is shown on the following chart. The first-listed text occurred immediately after Best left work, apparently while he was still at the YMCA, and the three texts in boldface type are those that were exchanged while Best was driving:

Sent	Sender	Received	Recipient
5:42:03	Best	5:42:12	Colonna
5:47:49	**Best**	**5:47:56**	**Colonna**
5:48:14	**Colonna**	**5:48:23**	**Best**
5:48:58	**Best**	**5:49:07**	**Colonna**
(5:49:15	*911 Call)*		
5:49:20	Colonna	5:55:30	Best
5:54:08	Colonna	5:55:33	Best

This sequence indicates the precise time of the accident—within seconds of 5:48:58. Seventeen seconds elapsed from Best's sending a text to Colonna and the time of the 911 call after the accident. Those seconds had to include Best's stopping his vehicle, observing the injuries to the Kuberts, and dialing 911. It appears, therefore, that Best collided with the Kuberts' motorcycle immediately after sending a text at 5:48:58. It can be inferred that he sent that text in response to Colonna's text to him that he received twenty-five seconds earlier. Finally, it appears that Best initiated the texting with Colonna as he was about to and after he began to drive home.

Missing from the evidence is the content of the text messages. Plaintiffs were not able to obtain the messages Best and Colonna actually exchanged, and Best and Colonna did not provide that information in their depositions. The excerpts of Best's deposition that have been provided to us for this appeal do not include questions and answers about the content of his text messages with Colonna late that afternoon. When Colonna's deposition was taken sixteen months after the accident, she testified she did not remember her texts that day. Despite the fact that Best did not respond to her last two texts at 5:55 p.m., and despite her learning on the same evening that he had been involved in a serious accident minutes before he failed to respond to her, Colonna testified that she had "no idea" what the contents of her text messages with Best were that afternoon.

After plaintiffs learned of Colonna's involvement and added her to their lawsuit, she moved for summary judgment. Her attorney argued to the trial court that Colonna had no liability for the accident because she was not present at the scene, had no legal duty to avoid sending a text to Best when he was driving, and further, that she did not know he was driving. The trial judge reviewed the evidence and the arguments of the attorneys, conducted independent research on the law, and ultimately concluded that Colonna did not have a legal duty to avoid sending a text message to Best, even if she knew he was driving. The judge dismissed plaintiffs' claims against Colonna.

II.

On appeal before us, plaintiffs argue that Colonna is potentially liable to them if a jury finds that her texting was a proximate cause of the accident. They argue that she can be found liable because she aided and abetted Best's unlawful texting while he was driving, and also because she had an independent duty to avoid texting to a person who was driving a motor vehicle. They claim that a jury can infer from the evidence that Colonna knew Best was driving home from his YMCA job when she texted him at 5:48:14, less than a minute before the accident.

We are not persuaded by plaintiffs' arguments as stated, but we also reject defendant's argument that a sender of text messages never has a duty to avoid texting to a person driving a vehicle. We conclude that a person sending text messages has a duty not to text someone who is driving if the texter knows, or has special reason to know, the recipient will view the text while driving. But we also conclude that plaintiffs have not presented sufficient evidence to prove that Colonna had such knowledge when she texted Best immediately before the accident.

A.

We first address generally the nature of a duty imposed by the common law. In a lawsuit alleging that a defendant is liable to a plaintiff because of the defendant's negligent conduct, the plaintiff must prove four things: (1) that the defendant owed a duty of care to the plaintiff, (2) that the defendant breached that duty, (3) that the breach was a proximate cause of the plaintiff's injuries, and (4) that the plaintiff suffered actual compensable injuries as a result. * * * The plaintiff bears the burden of proving each of these four "core elements" of a negligence claim. * * *

Because plaintiffs in this case sued Best and eventually settled their claims against him, it is important to note that the law recognizes that more than one defendant can be the proximate cause of and therefore liable for causing injury. * * * Whether a duty exists to prevent harm is not controlled by whether another person also has a duty, even a greater duty, to prevent the same harm. If more than one defendant breached his or her duty and proximately caused the injuries, the jury at a trial may determine relative fault and assign a percentage of responsibility to each under our comparative negligence statutes, * * *.

"A duty is an obligation imposed by law requiring one party 'to conform to a particular standard of conduct toward another.'" * * *

Whether a duty of care exists "is generally a matter for a court to decide," not a jury. * * * The "fundamental question [is] whether the plaintiff's interests are entitled to legal protection against the defendant's conduct." * * *

The New Jersey Supreme Court recently analyzed the common law process by which a court decides whether a legal duty of care exists to prevent injury to another. * * * The Court reviewed precedents developed over the years in our courts and restated the "most cogent explanation of the principles that guide [the courts] in determining whether to recognize the existence of a duty of care":

"[w]hether a person owes a duty of reasonable care toward another turns on whether the imposition of such a duty satisfies an abiding sense of basic fairness under all of the circumstances in light of considerations of public policy. That inquiry involves identifying, weighing, and balancing several factors—the relationship of the parties, the nature of the attendant risk, the opportunity and ability to exercise care, and the public interest in the proposed solution. . . . The analysis is both very fact-specific and principled; it must lead to solutions that properly and fairly resolve the specific case and generate intelligible and sensible rules to govern future conduct." * * *

The Court emphasized that the law must take into account "generally applicable rules to govern societal behaviors," not just an "outcome that reaches only the particular circumstances and parties before the Court today [.]" * * * The Court described all of these considerations as "a full duty analysis" to determine whether the law recognizes a duty of care in the particular circumstances of a negligence case. * * *

B.

In this case, plaintiffs argue that a duty of care should be imposed upon Colonna because she aided and abetted Best's violation of the law when he used his cell phone while driving. To support their argument, plaintiffs cite section 876 of the *Restatement (Second) of Torts* (1965), a compilation of common law principles. Under section 876 of the *Restatement,* an individual is liable if he or she knows that another person's "conduct constitutes a breach of duty and gives substantial assistance or encouragement to the other."

To illustrate this concept, the *Restatement* provides the following hypothetical example:

> A and B participate in a riot in which B, although throwing no rocks himself, encourages A to throw rocks. One of the rocks strikes C, a bystander. B is subject to liability to C. [*Restatement* § 876, comment d, illustration 4.]

The example illustrates that one does not actually have to be the person who threw a rock to be liable for injury caused by the rock. * * * In this case, plaintiffs assert that Colonna and Best were acting in concert in exchanging text messages. Although Colonna was at a remote location from the site of the accident, plaintiffs say she was "electronically present" in Best's pick-up truck immediately before the accident and she aided and abetted his unlawful use of his cell phone. * * *

In this case, Colonna did not have a special relationship with Best by which she could control his conduct. Nor is there evidence that she actively encouraged him to text her while he was driving. Colonna sent two texts to Best in the afternoon of September 21, 2009, one about two hours and the second about twenty-five seconds before the accident. What she said in those texts is unknown. Even if a reasonable inference can be drawn that she sent messages requiring responses, the act of sending such messages, by itself, is not active encouragement that the recipient read the text and respond immediately, that is, while driving and in violation of the law.

[T]he evidence in this case is not sufficient for a jury to conclude that Colonna took affirmative steps and gave substantial assistance to Best in violating the law. Plaintiffs produced no evidence tending to show that Colonna urged Best to read and respond to her text while he was driving.

The evidence available to plaintiffs is not sufficient to prove Colonna's liability to the Kuberts on the basis of aiding and abetting Best's negligent driving while using a cell phone.

C.

Plaintiffs argue alternatively that Colonna independently had a duty not to send texts to a person who she knew was driving a vehicle. They have not cited a case in New Jersey or any other jurisdiction that so holds, and we have not found one in our own research.

The trial court cited one case that involved distraction of the driver by text messages, * * * We view [this authority] as appropriately leading to the conclusion that one should not be held liable for sending a wireless transmission simply because some recipient might use his cell phone unlawfully and become distracted while driving. Whether by text, email, Twitter, or other means, the mere sending of a wireless transmission that unidentified drivers may receive and view is not enough to impose liability.

Having considered the competing arguments of the parties, we also conclude that liability is not established by showing only that the sender directed the message to a specific identified recipient, even if the sender knew the recipient was then driving. We conclude that additional proofs are necessary to establish the sender's liability, namely, that the sender also knew or had special reason to know that the driver would read the message while driving and would thus be distracted from attending to the road and the operation of the vehicle. * * *

A section of the *Restatement* that the parties have not referenced provides:

> An act is negligent if the actor intends it to affect, or realizes or should realize that it is likely to affect, the conduct of another, a third person, or an animal in such a manner as to create an unreasonable risk of harm to the other. [*Restatement* § 303.]

To illustrate this concept, the *Restatement* provides the following hypothetical example:

> A is driving through heavy traffic. B, a passenger in the back seat, suddenly and unnecessarily calls out to A, diverting his attention, thus causing him to run into the car of C. B is negligent toward C. * * *

We have recognized that a passenger who distracts a driver can be held liable for the passenger's own negligence in causing an accident. In other words, a passenger in a motor vehicle has a duty "not to interfere with the driver's operations." * * *

One form of interference with a driver might be obstructing his view or otherwise diverting his attention from the tasks of driving. It would be reasonable to hold a passenger liable for causing an accident if the passenger obstructed the driver's view of the road, for example, by suddenly holding a piece of paper in front of the driver's face and urging the driver to look at what is written or depicted on the paper. The same can be said if a passenger were to hold a cell phone with a text message or a picture in front of the driver's eyes. Such distracting conduct would be direct, independent negligence of the passenger, not aiding and abetting of the driver's negligent conduct. Here, of course, Colonna did not hold Best's cell phone in front of his eyes and physically distract his view of the road.

The more relevant question is whether a passenger can be liable not for actually obstructing the driver's view but only for urging the driver to take his eyes off the road and to look at a distracting object. We think the answer is yes, but only if the passenger's conduct is unreasonably risky because the passenger knows, or has special reason to know, that the driver will in fact be distracted and drive negligently as a result of the passenger's actions.

It is the primary responsibility of the driver to obey the law and to avoid distractions. Imposing a duty on a passenger to avoid any conduct that might theoretically distract the driver would open too broad a swath of potential liability in ordinary and innocent circumstances. [C]ourts must be careful not to "create a broadly worded duty and . . . run the risk of unintentionally imposing liability in situations far beyond the parameters we now face." "The scope of a duty is determined under 'the totality of the circumstances,' and must be 'reasonable' under those circumstances." * * *

"Foreseeability of the risk of harm is the foundational element in the determination of whether a duty exists." * * * "Foreseeability, in turn, is based on the defendant's knowledge of the risk of injury." * * *

It is foreseeable that a driver who is actually distracted by a text message might cause an accident and serious injuries or death, but it is not generally foreseeable that every recipient of a text message who is driving will neglect his obligation to obey the law and will be distracted by the text. Like a call to voicemail or an answering machine, the sending of a text message by itself does not demand that the recipient take any action. The sender should be able to assume that the recipient will read a text message only when it is safe and legal to do so, that is, when not operating a vehicle. However, if the sender knows that the recipient is both driving and will read the text immediately, then the sender has taken a foreseeable risk in sending a text at that time. The sender has knowingly engaged in distracting conduct, and it is not unfair also to hold the sender responsible for the distraction.

"When the risk of harm is that posed by third persons, a plaintiff may be required to prove that defendant was in a position to 'know or have reason to know, from past experience, that there [was] a likelihood of conduct on the part of [a] third person[ ]' that was 'likely to endanger the safety' of another." * * * [W]hen the sender "has actual knowledge or special reason to know," * * *, from prior texting experience or otherwise, that the recipient will view the text while driving, the sender has breached a duty of care to the public by distracting the driver.

Our conclusion that a limited duty should be imposed on the sender is supported by the "full duty analysis" described by the Supreme Court—identifying, weighing, and balancing "the relationship of the parties, the nature of the attendant risk, the opportunity and ability to exercise care, and the public interest in the proposed solution." * * * When the sender knows that the text will reach the driver while operating a vehicle, the sender has a relationship to the public who use the roadways similar to that of a passenger physically present in the vehicle. As we have stated, a passenger must avoid distracting the driver. The remote sender of a text who knows the recipient is then driving must do the same.

When the sender texts a person who is then driving, knowing that the driver will immediately view the text, the sender has disregarded the attendant and foreseeable risk of harm to the public. The risk is substantial, as evidenced by the dire consequences in this and similar cases where texting drivers have caused severe injuries or death.

With respect to the sender's opportunity to exercise care, "[a] corresponding consideration is the practicality of preventing [the risk]." * * * We must take into account "how establishing this duty will work in practice." * * * "When the defendant's actions are 'relatively easily corrected' and the harm sought to be presented is 'serious,' it is fair to impose a duty." * * *

At the same time, "[c]onsiderations of fairness implicate the scope as well as the existence of a duty." * * * Limiting the duty to persons who have such knowledge will not require that the sender of a text predict in every instance how a recipient will act. It will not interfere with use of text messaging to a driver that one expects will obey the law. The limited duty we impose will not hold texters liable for the unlawful conduct of others, but it will hold them liable for their own negligence when they have knowingly disregarded a foreseeable risk of serious injury to others.

Finally, the public interest requires fair measures to deter dangerous texting while driving. Just as the public has learned the dangers of drinking and driving through a sustained campaign and enhanced criminal penalties and civil liability, the hazards of texting when on the road, or to someone who is on the road, may become part of the public consciousness when the liability of those involved matches the seriousness of the harm.

Our concurring colleague expresses reluctance to conclude that a remote texter has an independent duty of care to avoid being a cause of traffic accidents and injuries. The concurring opinion states that traditional tort principles are sufficient to decide in this case that Colonna had no liability for the Kuberts' injuries and we should say no more. * * * We have been asked to decide the status of the law in these circumstances, and we have applied traditional tort principles, as developed in analogous cases, to delineate the limited scope of a remote texter's duty. "It has long been true that '[d]eterminations of the scope of duty in negligence cases has traditionally been a function of the judiciary.'" * * *

To summarize our conclusions, we do not hold that someone who texts to a person driving is liable for that person's negligent actions; the driver bears responsibility for obeying the law and maintaining safe control of the vehicle. We hold that, when a texter knows or has special reason to know that the intended recipient is driving and is likely to read the text message while driving, the texter has a duty to users of the public roads to refrain from sending the driver a text at that time.

D.

In this case, plaintiffs developed evidence pertaining to the habits of Best and Colonna in texting each other repeatedly. They also established that the day of the accident was not an unusual texting day for the two. But they failed to develop evidence tending to prove that Colonna not only knew that Best was driving when she texted him at 5:48:14 p.m. but that she knew he would violate the law and immediately view and respond to her text.

As our recitation of the facts shows, Colonna sent only one text while Best was driving. The contents of that text are unknown. No testimony established that she was aware Best would violate the law and read her text as he was driving, or that he would respond immediately. The evidence of multiple texting at other times when Best was not driving did not prove that Colonna breached the limited duty we have described.

Because the necessary evidence to prove breach of the remote texter's duty is absent on this record, summary judgment was properly granted dismissing plaintiffs' claims against Colonna.

Affirmed.

V.   THE SIMULATION EXERCISE

Your simulation exercise is to argue or oppose a Motion for Summary Judgment regarding Wendy Wife's liability to the plaintiffs injured by Harold at the shooting range. In Chapter 1 you considered only intentional tort claims arising from the case facts. There are also negligence claims to consider.

Assume that the injured and deceased parties have collectively sued Wendy for negligence alleging that she owed a duty to the victims because she knew about Harold's propensity for violent outbursts and she nonetheless sent the message when he was at the gun range. Plaintiffs argue that Wendy owed them a duty of care and that her breach caused their injuries.

Wendy Wife is moving the court for summary judgment on the duty of care element of the negligence claim. If her motion is granted, the judge will dismiss the case without holding a trial because no duty was owed. Wendy is arguing that she owed no duty of care and the case should be dismissed. The plaintiffs challenge that she did owe a duty of care and that the case should proceed to trial.

The judge will grant a motion for summary judgment if the moving party demonstrates that there is no genuine issue of material fact and the party is entitled to judgment as a matter of law. This standard is from Rule 56 of the Federal Rules of Civil Procedure provided in your materials.

This procedural context positions the parties to dispute the legal consequences of agreed-upon facts. Your professor will assign you teams so that separate groups argue both sides of this motion. Your task is to take the substantive duty of care rules introduced in *Kubert* and argue whether this case should be dismissed because no duty was owed using the facts in sections I and II. You may also draw upon the facts of Chapter 1 as well. You will have some time to prepare arguments in small groups and then advocates will model the motion argument before the class.

Consider how you can invoke policy arguments to support your side. For the defendant, what values are at stake in imposing a duty of care on Wendy? How might imposing a duty of care in this case go too far or raise concerns about the scope of tort liability? For the plaintiffs, how might imposing a duty of care here create a better society or support community-based values?

CHAPTER 5

NEGLIGENCE: DAMAGES

I. INTRODUCTION

While most tort law casebooks traditionally introduce damages hundreds of pages deep into the material, damages are actually both the beginning and the end of the case for clients and lawyers alike. The prospect of recovery for the plaintiff and the risk of financial loss for the defendant will often dictate which lawyers will take cases, whether cases settle, and how much time is invested in cases.

Understanding the depth and degree of your client's harms is central to tort lawyering. For the plaintiff, counsel will likely be working on a contingency fee basis. The lawyer will not be paid unless and until the plaintiff recovers. Plaintiffs' lawyers accordingly need to inquire early and often to understand the dollar value that might attach to a particular case. In many cases, this will be very difficult to quantify. What is the cost, for example, of a mother losing a child in active labor or of losing a loved one in a car accident? How does a lawyer convince a jury to put a dollar figure on that? If the plaintiff's counsel cannot expect to be made whole and make money off the case, counsel will likely not be willing to take the case. Consider carefully the implications of this. What types of injuries might never even be brought as lawsuits? What communities might be under-represented in tort litigation because of this financial structure?

For defendants, the threat of an adverse verdict may require financial planning, insurance consultation, and considerable defense costs, even if the defendant is ultimately found not liable. For defense counsel, it is incredibly challenging to contest the depth and extent of plaintiff's harms without crossing jury lines, such as appearing insensitive or callous. Managing emotions and empathy are thus a significant part of litigating damages for both sides.

Litigating damages requires several careful considerations. Lawyers have to cautiously advise clients given the uncertainty and indeterminacy in damage awards. In presenting a case to a jury, lawyers may have to navigate both deep emotional witness testimony, on the one extreme, and also technical and tedious expert testimony, on the other extreme.

Students will likely only study a half dozen or so damages cases in the course. Remember, however, that for all of the other cases you read throughout your course, intense and costly lawyering went into the simple sentence that makes its way into an appellate case stating that the jury awarded a verdict of $X or that the appellate court overturned a jury award of $Y.

In this simulation exercise, you will practice developing damage demands at the outset of a case. Damages are like a large "bucketing" exercise where you link what happened to a person to a category of recoverable damages and then you count (or estimate) how much is in each bucket. This simulation exercise practices applying the various damage categories you have studied in your course by extracting damages from a client narrative, bucketing them appropriately, and tabulating them accurately.

This simulation exercise accurately positions damages as the driving force of a malpractice case from the initial client intake, consistent with lawyering in practice. It debunks the idea that damages are the end result of the case.

II. JOURNAL OF SAM KENNEDY

Dec. 29,

I can't believe that I had to miss Ella's second Christmas because I was in the hospital with this tooth infection. She's just now old enough to actually get into the presents and understand what's going on. I missed all of it. This is going to hurt for a while, inside and out.

My doctor says it's called paresthesia. I can barely pronounce it, but I sure feel it! It feels like a constant prickling sensation in my face and jaw line with some numbness. It reminds me of when your foot falls asleep, but it won't go away. All of this poking and prodding has caused nerve damage. It will likely recover, but that doesn't help me now as I have coffee embarrassingly dripping down my chin and endless discomfort.

To make things even worse, I look like a chipmunk in the annual family Christmas photo. My face is really swollen and you can tell how miserable I am from just a quick glance. I can't wait to see how much worse it looks when Mom has it blown up and framed for the family picture wall. I can't even enjoy holiday food with the family because I can only eat really soft, plain foods. This has been the worst Christmas ever. My whole face hurts and I'm still bleeding inside my mouth. When it rains, it really pours. It's beyond frustrating. I'm just ready for everything to be back to normal.

Jan. 14,

Once again, this stupid root canal that Dr. Ellington messed up is stressing me out. Not only did it ruin the Christmas holidays, now I had to take off work to have it fixed. I scheduled everything specifically around school, so I wouldn't have to take any time off for it. And now I have to do just that. I've now maxed out my sick days. What if Ella gets sick? I don't have any more days left and I don't know what I'm going to do. This has been the absolute worst. My face is still swollen and I'm still sore. When will this nightmare end?

III. BILLING RECORDS

 ELLINGTON FAMILY DENTISTRY

PATIENT NAME: Sam Kennedy
ADDRESS: 1119 Brookington Ave.
                 Palsgraf, Tortsylvania 41578
PHONE: (513) 499-5637
DOB: 7/9/1990
ACCT NO.:   80556-341

DATE OF SERVICE	Description	PRICE
12/8	Initial Patient Consultation	$375.00
12/8	X-ray imaging – 3 views	$678.43
12/8	Root canal – Lower right second molar	$2,392.40
12/8	Anesthesia (gas)	$316.87
	TOTAL:	$3,762.70

AMOUNT DUE: $3,762.70

Make all checks payable to Ellington Family Dentistry.

Thank you for your business!

*PALSGRAF APOTHECARY *

266 South Maple Street
Palsgraf, Tortsylvania
(513) 488-5543
Open Mon. thru Fri. 9:00 am to 8:00 pm
Sat. and Sun. 1:00 pm to 5:00 pm

PATIENT NAME: Sam Kennedy

ADDRESS: 1119 Brookington Ave.
                       Palsgraf, Tortsylvania

DOB: 7/9/1990

PHONE NUMBER: (513) 499-5637

DATE	PRESCRIBER	MEDICATION	QTY	REFILS	DIRECTIONS	PRICE
12-8	Taylor Ellington, DMD	Ibuprofen 800 mg	24	0	Take 1 every 4 to 6 hours as needed for pain	$23.32
TOTAL AMOUNT DUE					$23.32	

* PALSGRAF APOTHECARY *

266 South Maple Street
Palsgraf, Tortsylvania
(513) 488-5543
Open Mon. thru Fri. 9:00 am to 8:00 pm
Sat. and Sun. 1:00 pm to 5:00 pm

PATIENT NAME: Sam Kennedy

ADDRESS: 1119 Brookington Ave.
                  Palsgraf, Tortsylvania

DOB: 7/9/1990

PHONE NUMBER: (513) 499-5637

DATE	PRESCRIBER	MEDICATION	QTY	REFILS	DIRECTIONS	PRICE
12-26	Beth Morgan, M.D.	Amoxicillin 500 mg	14	0	Take 1 capsule twice a day for 7 days. Take with food.	$14.78
12-26	Beth Morgan, M.D.	Hydrocodone 5/325 mg	16	0	Take 1 capsule every 6 hours as needed for pain. Do not drive or operate heavy machinery. Avoid alcohol while on this medication.	$22.36
		TOTAL AMOUNT DUE				*$37.14*

PALSGRAF COMMUNITY HOSPITAL
2456 North Oak Street
Palsgraf, Tortsylvania 41578
Phone: (513) 498-0329
Fax: (513) 498-0770

DATE: 12/25

PATIENT INFORMATION:

TIME: 9:36 A.M.

Name:	Sam Kennedy
Address:	1119 Brookington Avenue
	Palsgraf, Tortsylvania 41578
Phone Number:	(513) 499-5637
Date of Birth:	July 9, 1990
Age:	28 years old
Height:	5'5"
Emergency Contact:	Evelyn Kennedy
Relationship to Patient:	Mother
Occupation:	Teacher
Employer:	Palsgraf Middle School
Work Phone Number:	(513) 498-0038
PCP:	Dr. Ronald Smith, M.D.

DISCHARGE INSTRUCTIONS:

You have been treated for a dental infection and discharged with 2 prescriptions. Take all medicine as directed. If your symptoms worsen, call your primary care physician immediately. Follow up with dentist as planned.

DATE OF SERVICE	DESCRIPTION	PROVIDER	COST
12/23	Emergency Room Visit – Level 4	Dr. Shay Roberson, M.D.	$3,975.45
12/23	X-rays	Dr. Shay Roberson, M.D.	$937.08
12/23	CBC Lab Work	Dr. Shay Roberson, M.D.	$97.46
12/23 - 12/25	2-day hospital Admission	Dr. Beth Morgan, M.D.	$29,460.12
		TOTAL DUE	**$34,470.11**

Dr. Rachel Salyer, DMD, MS
2789 Dogwood Lane, Suite 425
Clarksville, Tortsylvania 45624
Phone: (513) 635-3773
Fax: (513) 635-3992

PATIENT NAME: Sam Kennedy
ADDRESS: 1119 Brookington Avenue
CITY, STATE, ZIP: Palsgraf, Tortslyvania 41578
PHONE: (513) 499-5637
DOB: 7/9/1990
ACCOUNT NO.:   1982038

Date of Service	Description	Price
12/27	Initial Consultation	$500.00
12/27	X-Ray Imaging	$763.47
12/27	Retrieval of instrument and treatment of infected molar	$1,983.64
TOTAL AMOUNT		$3,247.11

PAY THIS AMOUNT: $3,247.11

Clarksville Endodontics

Dr. Rachel Salyer, DMD, MS
2789 Dogwood Lane, Suite 425
Clarksville, Tortsylvania 45624
Phone: (513) 635-3773
Fax: (513) 635-3992

PATIENT NAME: Sam Kennedy
ADDRESS: 1119 Brookington Avenue
CITY, STATE, ZIP: Palsgraf, Tortsylvania 41578
PHONE: (513) 499-5637
DOB: 7/9/1990
ACCOUNT NO.:   1982038

Date of Service	Description	Price
12/28	Office Visit – Established Patient	$150.00
12/28	X-Ray Imaging	$763.47
12/28	Anesthesia	$478.92
12/28	Root canal, Lower right 2nd molar	$4,589.87
	TOTAL AMOUNT	$5,982.26

PAY THIS AMOUNT: **$5,982.26**

Dr. Rachel Salyer, DMD, MS
2789 Dogwood Lane, Suite 425
Clarksville, Tortsylvania 45624
Phone: (513) 635-3773
Fax: (513) 635-3992

PATIENT NAME:	*Sam Kennedy*
ADDRESS:	*1119 Brookington Avenue*
CITY, STATE, ZIP:	*Palsgraf, Tortslyvania 41578*
PHONE:	*(513) 499-5637*
DOB:	*7/9/1990*
ACCOUNT NO.:	*1982038*

Date of Service	Description	Price
1/3	Office Visit – Established Patient	$150.00
1/3	X-Ray Imaging	$763.47
1/3	Anesthesia	$478.92
1/3	Crown, Lower right 2nd molar	$3,859.27
TOTAL AMOUNT		**$5,251.66**

PAY THIS AMOUNT: $5,251.66

IV. THE SIMULATION EXERCISE

Your client is Sam Kennedy. Sam has delivered the above receipts and journal entries to your office documenting the out-of-pocket expenses to date in the case against Dr. Ellington and/or the product manufacturer of the dental file. Your supervising partner has asked you to tabulate the receipts and calculate the out-of-pocket expenses. Prepare a chart calculating the total amount of damages for both past medical costs and lost wages.

Pain and suffering damages are another critical category of recovery. Review the facts presented in the client's journal and in the standard of care chapter (Chapter 2) to identify facts supporting a pain and suffering damages recovery for the plaintiff. Email your supervising partner previewing the facts supporting a high possible range of recovery for Sam's pain and suffering.

Strategize how to tell the story of pain and suffering to a jury. Brainstorm what other evidence you might be able to develop with Sam to support a pain and suffering verdict. What kinds of questions would you ask in Sam's deposition or trial testimony to develop pain and suffering facts?

As you work through this simulation assignment, note the stark differences between lawyering out-of-pocket damages and non-economic damages. These damage categories differ greatly in the likelihood of recovery and the method of proof. One is highly technical and mathematical. The other is highly emotive and subjective.

You should draft an email to the supervising partner with both the calculations chart and your pain and suffering analysis.

~ 53,000 past medical

~150 x 4 = 600 future medical

5,000 er visits.

special

~~37 yrs work X 61,390 = 2.27 million~~

30 days   42,000 yr = 4K ~~future~~ lost wage

37 yrs X 42000 yr = 1.5 mil ~~lost~~ future

nonspecial

missing Christmas

pain suffering = 160,000

CHAPTER 6

OWNERS AND OCCUPIERS OF LAND LIABILITY

I. INTRODUCTION

This chapter introduces the standards of care governing particular owner and occupier relationships. It is an engaging unit to consider the relative power that landowners have in tort law compared to other categories of defendants. This unit can reveal societal privileges and social norms quite vividly.

To see the architecture of this unit, it can be very helpful to map out the categories of liability in a chart. For each category that you study (e.g., trespassers, social guests, business guests, tenants), consider what the relationship is, what legal rules apply to that relationship, how the rules have changed over time, and what rationales support the rules. This is a dynamic unit to link legal rules to their underlying policy rationales and critiques.

Think about this material through the imagery of the various "hats" that each individual in a claim wore at the time of the tort relative to the defendant(s). For example, if someone slips and falls in the local ice cream shop, some individuals in the shop might be patrons, others might be trespassers, others might be employees. The starting point to a successful analysis is accurately identifying the respective relationships between plaintiffs and defendants and applying the standards of care that govern those relationships. Social guests, business guests, trespassers, and landlords are the statuses that you are most likely to study. Every year this content gets more interesting though as we move into a world of VRBO and Airbnb in which these clearly defined relationship categories are blurring considerably.

Most of the material studied in your primary casebook on this topic is really only addressing whether a duty of care was owed and whether a standard of care was breached. Remember that lawyers will still need to proceed through a full causation and damages analysis as well after establishing duty and breach.

This simulation assignment returns you to our Sharp Shooter's fact pattern to consider whether the business holds any tort liability for the harms that occurred. Think about pragmatic lawyering strategies here. While we brainstormed many possible intentional torts claims against the shooter in Chapter 1, it is quite possible that the business premises is the most financially viable defendant from which the plaintiffs can recover. It is unlikely that either the husband (Chapter 1) or the wife (Chapter 4) have the financial means to make the plaintiffs whole given the complexities of their legal issues and the extent of the harm suffered.

The following materials reveal a possible theory of negligence liability against Sharp Shooter's. You represent the plaintiffs who were harmed in the shooting (not the shooter, Harold, although he was also harmed). Your firm has hired a potential expert witness to study the premises to determine whether the gun range complied with governing standards of care. This is an expensive undertaking to build a case. Your firm is likely paying out of pocket to investigate this case.

These facts build on the case file introduced in Chapter 1. Chapter 1 explained how the shooting occurred, who was harmed, and how. The potential expert witness will reveal how the gun range construction and design could have protected some of the plaintiffs more effectively. You will draft a complaint pleading this new cause of action against the business premises defendant.

II. INTERVIEW NOTES

Today I met with Remington Wesson, founder, president, and CEO of Safety First Range, Inc. I explained that I represent the plaintiffs suing Sharp Shooter's Gun Range. I explained that I am looking to retain an expert in the case. Before our meeting, Wesson had visited Sharp Shooter's Gun Range and reviewed the police report.

Wesson founded Safety First Range (SFR) five years ago to promote safety in gun ranges. SFR is leading the way in research and development of gun range safety standards. It assists clients in designing and constructing their gun ranges to be as safe as possible for customers.

Wesson started going to various shooting ranges when he was a police officer. He retired from the police force after 25 years and decided to open SFR after years of observing the absence of standardized safety protocols for ranges. He started SFR to create "best practices" to enhance safety and uniformity.

He explained that he has created the "gold standard" that is followed by a large majority of gun ranges nationwide. SFR has conducted research and published findings outlining these safety standards.

Wesson concluded preliminarily that Sharp Shooter's Gun Range was not designed consistent with safety standards in the industry. During his inspection of the premises, he noticed several deficiencies with how the shooting stalls were designed, including the material used for the barriers between the stalls, the height of the barriers, and the width of the barriers.

We walked through his notes from that initial site inspection. He explained that the barriers installed at the range were made of plywood that was only one-inch thick. There were bullet holes in the plywood indicating that errant bullets had penetrated the barrier.

Wesson showed me a diagram he had prepared. This drawing depicted how layers of steel core barriers should have been installed between stalls to prevent penetration.

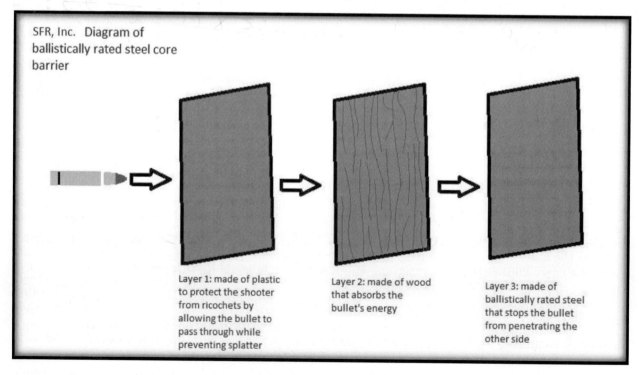

SFR, Inc. Diagram of ballistically rated steel core barrier

Layer 1: made of plastic to protect the shooter from ricochets by allowing the bullet to pass through while preventing splatter

Layer 2: made of wood that absorbs the bullet's energy

Layer 3: made of ballistically rated steel that stops the bullet from penetrating the other side

He explained that, in a well-designed gun range, the barriers between the shooting stalls should be made of a ballistically rated steel core containing three layers to prevent the bullets from penetrating the barrier. The first layer is made of plastic which protects the shooter from ricochets by allowing the bullet to pass through while preventing splatter. The second layer is made of wood that absorbs the bullet's energy. The last layer is ballistic steel that stops the bullet so that it does not go through to the other side and enter the next stall.

I asked him if this type of barrier could have prevented injuries in this case. He thought that improved barrier construction would have prevented injury to Ervin Employee and Gertrude Guest. His conclusion was based on his observation of bullet holes in the plywood barrier that separated Harold's shooting stall from where Ervin Employee and Gertrude Guest were located. Because there was not a sufficient barrier between the stalls, the errant bullets penetrated the plywood barrier between the stalls and injured Ervin and Gertrude. This could have been prevented if the barriers were designed to stop the bullet, like the ballistically rated steel core barriers.

Wesson also identified concerns with the height of the barriers. He prepared the below image demonstrating the recommended construction height of the barriers between stalls. It shows the insufficient height of the barriers between shooting stalls at Sharp Shooter's.

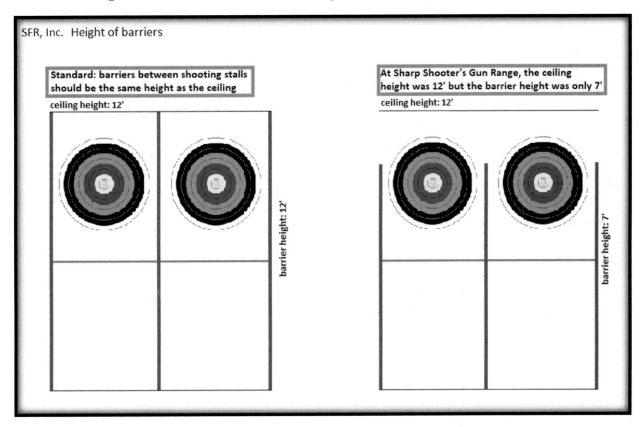

Wesson concluded that the barriers should extend all the way to the ceiling to prevent errant bullets from entering a different shooting stall. When the barriers do not extend all the way up to the ceiling, then patrons and employees in other stalls are exposed to bullet ricochets and the risk of injury increases.

Wesson measured the trajectory of the bullets based on the marks on the ceiling. Wesson preliminarily concluded that after Harold Husband fired the shot in the air, the bullet hit the ceiling and ricocheted downward. Since the barrier between the stall was only 7 feet high, the bullet passed, unhindered, into lane 2 and struck Damien. This could have been prevented if the barriers between the stalls extended all the way to the ceiling. The barrier would have stopped the errant bullet from entering the adjacent stall.

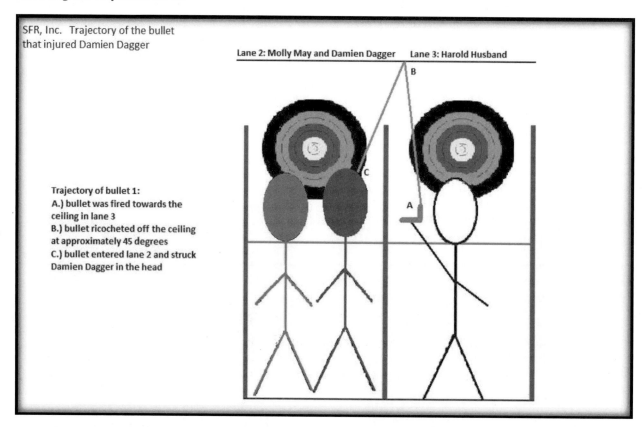

SFR, Inc.   Trajectory of the bullet that injured Damien Dagger

Lane 2: Molly May and Damien Dagger   Lane 3: Harold Husband

Trajectory of bullet 1:
A.) bullet was fired towards the ceiling in lane 3
B.) bullet ricocheted off the ceiling at approximately 45 degrees
C.) bullet entered lane 2 and struck Damien Dagger in the head

Wesson concluded that the Sharp Shooter's Gun Range was not reasonably safe for customers consistent with industry practices. He concluded that injuries could have been prevented if these safety measures were put in place.

We further discussed the scope and terms of representation. I agreed to send him a retainer letter for review by next week.

III. LEGAL RESEARCH

Below is a short excerpt from the Federal Rules of Civil Procedure. These rules advise you how to style and structure facts into a civil complaint for relief. These rules might also be used to inform your brainstorming of what facts yield viable causes of action. This is the same procedural context governing your complaint drafting in Chapter 1.

These are both federal rules that would apply in federal court. In civil procedure you will study whether a lawsuit should be filed in federal or state court. Many tort law cases will be state cases applying state rules of procedure. The federal rules are used for this simulation because it likely reinforces your civil procedure course content.

Rule 8. General Rules of Pleading

(a)   Claim for Relief. A pleading that states a claim for relief must contain:

(1)   a short and plain statement of the grounds for the court's jurisdiction, unless the court already has jurisdiction and the claim needs no new jurisdictional support;

(2)   a short and plain statement of the claim showing that the pleader is entitled to relief; and

(3)   a demand for the relief sought, which may include relief in the alternative or different types of relief.

Rule 10. Form of Pleadings

(a)   Caption; Names of Parties. Every pleading must have a caption with the court's name, a title, [and] a file number. . . The title of the complaint must name all the parties; the title of other pleadings, after naming the first party on each side, may refer generally to other parties.

(b)   Paragraphs; Separate Statements. A party must state its claims or defenses in numbered paragraphs, each limited as far as practicable to a single set of circumstances. A later pleading may refer by number to a paragraph in an earlier pleading.

IV. THE SIMULATION EXERCISE

Complaint drafting is the threshold lawyering task to initiate a lawsuit. In Chapter 1, you drafted a complaint alleging intentional tort claims against Harold Husband. That drafting simulation left the claims against the Sharp Shooter's entity unaddressed. It is now time to plead a claim against the business premises. Draft a civil complaint alleging premises liability claims against the Sharp Shooter's Gun Range. Remember that this is your first pleading in a case. The facts will be developed much more thoroughly through discovery. At this early stage, you are ensuring that you have a well-plead complaint sufficient to withstand a motion to dismiss.

Use the key cases from your primary textbook to extract the rule governing business premises liability. You will then tether the elements of a premises liability claim to the facts presented in this chapter. You will begin by identifying who can sue the premises based on the facts provided. Consider carefully the different "hats" everyone is wearing. Ervin, the employee, for example, may have different claims than the patrons of the gun range. Which injuries were actually caused by the conduct of the business premises? Which breaches caused which plaintiff's injuries?

CHAPTER 7

WRONGFUL DEATH AND SURVIVAL

I. INTRODUCTION

The wrongful death and survival unit is often one of the hardest for students to conceptualize. The law varies considerably from jurisdiction to jurisdiction and it is often governed by statute. Wrongful death and survival concepts also tether to most tort law causes of action whether the underlying claim is an intentional tort, a products liability claim, or a malpractice case, thus creating layers of complexity.

Survival claims consider whether the deceased can recover for the harms that they suffered while alive. In other words, can the deceased's estate sue on its behalf to recover damages that the deceased incurred directly. This can include damage categories such as past medical expenses, lost wages, property damage, and past pain and suffering. A survival claim—as the title suggests—gets at whether a claim survives death. Most tort claims survive death today. Defamation, discussed in Chapter 12, would be the one narrow exception. Reputational harms generally do not survive death, although there are some exceptions.

Historically, tort claims died with the decedent. This created a perverse and morbid policy framework whereby a defendant would pay more in damages to an injured plaintiff than to a deceased plaintiff. We are so far removed from this historic context though that law students in my year-long torts class, in which wrongful death is covered in the spring semester, never even pause or hesitate to bring claims in which the plaintiff is deceased a full semester before learning the legal rules that support this conclusion.

Survival claims alone, however, can leave the financial dependents of the decedent in a difficult situation if they were dependent on the income, love, and affection of the deceased while alive. The loss of their loved one costs them a relationship and resources. The survival claim will not allow recovery for the losses that surviving loved ones suffered because survival claims are only plead on behalf of the deceased for harms to the deceased.

This critical gap is where the wrongful death statute comes in to fill the void. Wrongful death claims consider whether loved ones of the deceased are able to sue for the losses that they suffered. The litigants are notably different in the two claims. The estate of the deceased is bringing the survival claim. The qualifying beneficiaries of the deceased are bringing wrongful death claims. This can be confusing because the same person might wear two entirely separate plaintiff hats. A wife might be representing the estate standing in for the deceased. A wife might also be a qualifying beneficiary bringing her own claim for her losses as a wife.

The wrongful death statute answers critical questions regarding who can sue, how much can be recovered, and by when they must sue. These answers can be surprising (e.g., damage caps), so review your local law carefully. Qualifying beneficiaries are typically legal and biological loved ones only. This is a statutorily defined group of claimants. The qualifying beneficiaries must prove that the defendant caused the death of their loved one through a wrongful act. Damages are usually for economic losses and loss of comfort, society, and companionship. There are real proof challenges considering what someone's earnings might have been into the future and real lawyering challenges attaching a dollar figure to a lost relationship.

The two claims can go together if the tort caused the death, but they need not. For example, if a plaintiff slips and falls on a banana peel at the grocery store and suffers a sprained back, she has a possible negligence suit against the premises. If, before she recovers in a successful suit against the grocer, she subsequently dies from cancer unrelated to the fall, then she has a survival claim, but no wrongful death claim accrues for her qualifying beneficiaries because the tort did not cause her death.

For an example of how the two claims interrelate, consider—tragically—the facts that arise in far too many mass shooting incidents. The news reports on the day of the tragedy that there were six immediate deaths. Two days later, the news reports that an additional victim has died from her wounds. The qualifying beneficiaries of the immediate decedents are all entitled to bring wrongful death suits, but if a victim died instantaneously, there may not be a substantial survival claim because the deceased may not have medical expenses or sustained pain and suffering. The victim who lived for a few days and then died would recover the medical expenses and pain and suffering from those surviving days in a survival claim. Qualifying beneficiaries would also hold a wrongful death claim for their lost economic support and lost companionship.

This chapter challenges you to construct wrongful death and survival claims precisely and accurately. In Chapter 1, you brainstormed claims arising from the incident involving Harold Husband at the Sharp Shooter's range. In Chapter 6, you also pursued claims against the business premises. You have already filed these suits. It is becoming increasingly clear though that Harold is not a very financially viable defendant.

You will now reach out to defense counsel while the case is underway to try to persuade the defendant to settle. This will require you to precisely identify who has claims for what damages. This requires discerning who lived, who died, who suffered, and who incurred medical expenses. It also requires discerning who holds relationships that support a wrongful death claim. You will learn more in the subsequent materials about how they suffered, what their income was, and who their loved ones were.

———————

II. SUPPORTING DOCUMENTS

U.S. STANDARD CERTIFICATE OF DEATH

1. DECEDENT'S LEGAL NAME (Include AKA's if any) (First, Middle, Last) Molly Marie May	2. SEX Female	3. SOCIAL SECURITY NUMBER █████████

4. State I.D. 93456	5. DATE OF BIRTH (Mo/Day/Yr) 02/04/57	6. BIRTHPLACE (City and State or Foreign Country) Palsgraf, Tortsylvania

7a. RESIDENCE-STATE Tortsylvania	7b. COUNTY Palsgraf	7c. CITY OR TOWN Palsgraf

7d. STREET AND NUMBER 2700 Melinda Court	7e. APT. NO. 2E	7f. ZIP CODE 12345	7g. INSIDE CITY LIMITS? ☑ Yes ☐ No

8. EVER IN US ARMED FORCES? ☐ Yes ☑ No	9. MARITAL STATUS AT TIME OF DEATH ☐ Married ☐ Married, but separated ☐ Widowed ☐ Divorced ☑ Never Married ☐ Unknown	10. SURVIVING SPOUSE'S NAME (If wife, give name prior to first marriage) None

11. FATHER'S NAME (First, Middle, Last) Robert Clarence May (deceased)	12. MOTHER'S NAME PRIOR TO FIRST MARRIAGE (First, Middle, Last) Rhonda Degrasse (deceased)

13a. INFORMANT'S NAME Clayton Brown	13b. RELATIONSHIP TO DECEDENT Police officer	13c. MAILING ADDRESS (Street and Number, City, State, Zip Code) 102 Siren Lane, Palsgraf, Tortsylvania 12345

14. PLACE OF DEATH (Check only one: see instructions)

IF DEATH OCCURRED IN A HOSPITAL: ☑ Inpatient ☐ Emergency Room/Outpatient ☐ Dead on Arrival	IF DEATH OCCURRED SOMEWHERE OTHER THAN A HOSPITAL: ☐ Hospice facility ☐ Nursing home/Long term care facility ☐ Decedent's home ☐ Other (Specify):

15. FACILITY NAME (If not institution, give street & number) Palsgraf Hospital	16. CITY OR TOWN, STATE, AND ZIP CODE Palsgraf, Tortsylvania 12345	17. COUNTY OF DEATH Palsgraf

18. METHOD OF DISPOSITION: ☐ Burial ☑ Cremation ☐ Donation ☐ Entombment ☐ Removal from State ☐ Other (Specify):	19. PLACE OF DISPOSITION (Name of cemetery, crematory, other place) Palsgraf Crematory

20. LOCATION-CITY, TOWN, AND STATE Palsgraf, Tortsylvania	21. NAME AND COMPLETE ADDRESS OF FUNERAL FACILITY Palsgraf Funeral Home 1847 Lily Ave., Palsgraf, Tortsylvania 12345

23. LICENSE NUMBER (Of Licensee) 07-11493

ITEMS 24-28 MUST BE COMPLETED BY PERSON WHO PRONOUNCES OR CERTIFIES DEATH	24. DATE PRONOUNCED DEAD (Mo/Day/Yr) 03/06	25. TIME PRONOUNCED DEAD 9:32pm

26. SIGNATURE OF PERSON PRONOUNCING DEATH (Only when applicable)	27. LICENSE NUMBER 495-0021	28. DATE SIGNED (Mo/Day/Yr) 03/06

29. ACTUAL OR PRESUMED DATE OF DEATH (Mo/Day/Yr) (Spell Month) March 6	30. ACTUAL OR PRESUMED TIME OF DEATH 9:32pm	31. WAS MEDICAL EXAMINER OR CORONER CONTACTED? ☑ Yes ☐ No

CAUSE OF DEATH (See instructions and examples)

32. PART I. Enter the chain of events--diseases, injuries, or complications--that directly caused the death. DO NOT enter terminal events such as cardiac arrest, respiratory arrest, or ventricular fibrillation without showing the etiology. DO NOT ABBREVIATE. Enter only one cause on a line. Add additional lines if necessary.

Approximate Interval: Onset to death

IMMEDIATE CAUSE (Final disease or condition ------->

a. Sepsis   resulting in death)

Due to (or as a consequence of):

Sequentially list conditions, if any, leading to the cause listed on line a. Enter the UNDERLYING CAUSE

b. Perforating non-contact wound to the chest

Due to (or as a consequence of):

c.

(disease or injury that initiated the events resulting in death) LAST

Due to (or as a consequence of):

d.

Left margin vertical text: To Be Completed/Verified By: FUNERAL DIRECTOR:

Left margin vertical text: To Be Completed By: MEDICAL CERTIFIER

| PART II. Enter other significant conditions contributing to death but not resulting in the underlying cause given in PART I | 33. WAS AN AUTOPSY PERFORMED? ☐ Yes ☑ No |
| | 34. WERE AUTOPSY FINDINGS AVAILABLE TO COMPLETE THE CAUSE OF DEATH? ☐ Yes ☐ No |

35. DID TOBACCO USE CONTRIBUTE TO DEATH?	36. IF FEMALE:	37. MANNER OF DEATH
☐ Yes ☐ Probably ☐ No ☑ Unknown	☑ Not pregnant within past year ☐ Pregnant at time of death ☐ Not pregnant, but pregnant within 42 days of death ☐ Not pregnant, but pregnant 43 days to 1 year before death ☐ Unknown if pregnant within the past year	☐ Natural ☐ Homicide ☑ Accident ☐ Pending Investigation ☐ Suicide ☐ Could not be determined

| 38. DATE OF INJURY (Mo/Day/Yr) (Spell Month)
March 4 | 39. TIME OF INJURY
11:45am | 40. PLACE OF INJURY (e.g., Decedent's home; construction site; restaurant; wooded area)
Gun range | 41. INJURY AT WORK?
☐ Yes ☑ No |

| 43. DESCRIBE HOW INJURY OCCURRED:
Hit by stray bullet discharged by shooting range patron's firearm | 44. IF TRANSPORTATION INJURY, SPECIFY:
☐ Driver/Operator
☐ Passenger
☐ Pedestrian
☐ Other (Specify) |

45. CERTIFIER (Check only one):
☐   Certifying physician-To the best of my knowledge, death occurred due to the cause(s) and manner stated.
☐   Pronouncing & Certifying physician-To the best of my knowledge, death occurred at the time, date, and place, and due to the cause(s) and manner stated.
☑   Medical Examiner/Coroner-On the basis of examination, and/or investigation, in my opinion, death occurred at the time, date, and place, and due to the cause(s) and manner stated.

Signature of certifier: _[signature]_

46. NAME, ADDRESS, AND ZIP CODE OF PERSON COMPLETING CAUSE OF DEATH (Item 32) Cory Coroner			
47. TITLE OF CERTIFIER County Coroner	48. LICENSE NUMBER 68225963C	49. DATE CERTIFIED (Mo/Day/Yr) 06/17/2004	50. FOR REGISTRAR ONLY- DATE FILED (Mo/Day/Yr)

Palsgraf Hospital

123 Emergency Street   564-444-0374
Pasigraf, Tortsylvania   www.palsgrafhospital.org
12345

BILLED TO
Molly May
2700 Melinda Court,
Apt. 2E
Palsgraf, Tortsylvania
12345

Invoice

INVOICE NUMBER
00074275

DATE OF ISSUE
03/31

DESCRIPTION	UNIT COST	QTY/HR RATE	AMOUNT
Room and Board – Semi Private	$60/hr	54 hr	$3,240.00
Intensive Care Unit	$625/hr	54 hr	$33,750.00
Pharmacy	Varies		$18,045.50
Medical/Surgical Supplies and Devices	Varies		$994.00
Laboratory	Varies		$8,335.50
Emergency Room	$700/hr	3 hr	$2,100.00
EKG/ECG	$400/ea	1 ea	$400

SUBTOTAL	$66,865.00
Insurance coverage	$53,492
(TAX RATE)	6%
TAX	$802.38

INVOICE TOTAL

$14,175.38

INVOICE TOTAL

$14,175.38

Please pay invoice within 30 days of invoice date

Anita Nicely, RN

Date	Observation
03/05 2130	Patient was brought to Emergency Room at 1245 in critical condition due to a perforating non-contact gunshot wound to the left side of her chest. She was stabilized and given a blood transfusion (2 pints, type AB negative). After transfusion patient was brought to ICU for further care and observation. On arrival, patient was under anesthesia. At approximately 2100, patient regained consciousness. Her breath became labored and she began to exhibit signs of distress. I assessed patient's pain levels (7 out of 10). I administered 2.5mg morphine intravenously. After approx. 15 minutes, patient began to exhibit signs of lessening pain.
03/05 2330	Checked on patient after morphine administration. Patient was confused and disoriented and complained of pain around the wound site and "inside her chest." I informed her that I could administer a maximum of 2.5mg morphine, but that more could not be administered for an additional three hours after that. Patient said she didn't care, she "just wanted it to stop hurting." I administered the additional 2.5mg morphine and stayed until patient began to settle.
03/06 0030	Patient was asleep, but restless. Checked all vitals. Heart rate slightly elevated (95bpm). Patient had temperature of 99.7°F. No family members have been identified yet.
03/06 0230	Patient was awake, restless, and disoriented. Patient's temperature increased to 100.2 °F. Checked wound dressing on left side of patient's chest. Wound site appeared reddened and slightly inflamed, with some discharge from the incision site. I noted on patient's chart and informed Dr. Dare. Dr. Dare administered 500mg doripenem (antibiotic) and 4mg morphine for pain.
03/06 0430	No change. Patient still exhibiting signs of pain. Vital signs stable.
03/06 0630	Patient was disoriented and exhibited signs of extreme pain and difficulty breathing. Wound site is inflamed and very red. Informed Dr. Dare. Dr. Dare intubated patient due to breathing difficulties and ordered blood tests for infection.
03/06 0830	Patient is stable. Heart rate is still high (105 bpm). Renal functions decreased. Hospital social worker is looking to determine next of kin.
03/06 0942	Patient blood pressure dropped to 30bpm. Patient had complete renal and respiratory failure. Dr. Dare and ICU team attempted resuscitation, but patient had entered septic shock. Patient time of death was 0932. Stepfather, Thomas Maynard, has been notified by hospital personnel. Maynard stated that he has not had contact with May since May's biological mother passed away several years ago, but he is the only next of kin.

MAY, MOLLY   ICU

Palsgraf Funeral Home   **INVOICE**

1847 Lily Avenue

Tortsylvania, 12345

INVOICE NO.   5944

DATE   March 9

CLIENT

Thomas Maynard

700 Steppe Road

Tortsylvania, 12345

	QTY	UNIT	ITEM	PRICE	TOTAL
MATERIALS			Basic cremation package	$1700.00	

	NAME	SERVICE	FEE	TOTAL
SERVICE				

MATERIALS	$1700.00
SERVICE	
TAX	$102.00
TOTAL	$1802.00

U.S. STANDARD CERTIFICATE OF DEATH

To Be Completed/ Verified By: FUNERAL DIRECTOR:

1. DECEDENT'S LEGAL NAME (Include AKA's if any) (First, Middle, Last) Damien Ray Dagger	2. SEX Male	3. SOCIAL SECURITY NUMBER xxx-xx-4721

4.. AGE-Last Birthday (Years) 37	5. DATE OF BIRTH (Mo/Day/Yr) 11/29/83	6. BIRTHPLACE (City and State or Foreign Country) Palsgraf, Tortsylvania

7a. RESIDENCE-STATE Tortsylvania	7b. COUNTY Palsgraf	7c. CITY OR TOWN Palsgraf

7d. STREET AND NUMBER 36 Sharpe Drive	7e. APT. NO.	7f. ZIP CODE 12345	7g. INSIDE CITY LIMITS? ☒ Yes ☐ No

8. EVER IN US ARMED FORCES? ☐ Yes ☐ No	9. MARITAL STATUS AT TIME OF DEATH ☒ Married ☐ Married, but separated ☐ Widowed ☐ Divorced ☐ Never Married ☐ Unknown	10. SURVIVING SPOUSE'S NAME (If wife, give name prior to first marriage) Deborah Reynolds

11. FATHER'S NAME (First, Middle, Last) Daryl Ray Dagger	12. MOTHER'S NAME PRIOR TO FIRST MARRIAGE (First, Middle, Last) Mary Scott

13a. INFORMANT'S NAME Clayton Brown	13b. RELATIONSHIP TO DECEDENT Police officer	13c. MAILING ADDRESS (Street and Number, City, State, Zip Code) 102 Siren Lane, Palsgraf, Tortsylvania 12345

14. PLACE OF DEATH (Check only one: see instructions)

15. FACILITY NAME (If not institution, give street & number) Sharp Shooter's Gun Range	16. CITY OR TOWN , STATE, AND ZIP CODE Palsgraf, Tortsylvania 12345	17. COUNTY OF DEATH Palsgraf

19. METHOD OF DISPOSITION: ☐ Burial ☐ Cremation ☐ Donation ☐ Entombment ☐ Removal from State ☐ Other (Specify):	19. PLACE OF DISPOSITION (Name of cemetery, crematory, other place) Palsgraf Cemetery

20. LOCATION-CITY, TOWN, AND STATE Palsgraf, Tortsylvania	21. NAME AND COMPLETE ADDRESS OF FUNERAL FACILITY Palsgraf Funeral Home 1847 Lily Ave., Palsgraf, Tortsylvania 12345

22. SIGNATURE OF FUNERAL SERVICE LICENSEE OR OTHER AGENT	23. LICENSE NUMBER (Of Licensee) 07-11493

To Be Completed By: MEDICAL CERTIFIER

ITEMS 24-28 MUST BE COMPLETED BY PERSON WHO PRONOUNCES OR CERTIFIES DEATH	24. DATE PRONOUNCED DEAD (Mo/Day/Yr) 03/04	25. TIME PRONOUNCED DEAD 12:23pm
26. SIGNATURE OF PERSON PRONOUNCING DEATH (Only when applicable)	27. LICENSE NUMBER 207-3994	28. DATE SIGNED (Mo/Day/Yr) 03/05

29. ACTUAL OR PRESUMED DATE OF DEATH (Mo/Day/Yr) (Spell Month) March 4	30. ACTUAL OR PRESUMED TIME OF DEATH 11:45am	31. WAS MEDICAL EXAMINER OR CORONER CONTACTED? ☐ Yes ☒ No

CAUSE OF DEATH (See instructions and examples)

Approximate interval: Onset to death

32. **PART I.** Enter the chain of events--diseases, injuries, or complications--that directly caused the death. DO NOT enter terminal events such as cardiac arrest, respiratory arrest, or ventricular fibrillation without showing the etiology. DO NOT ABBREVIATE. Enter only one cause on a line. Add additional lines if necessary.

IMMEDIATE CAUSE (Final disease or condition ———> a. Perforating non-contact wound to the head resulting in death)

Due to (or as a consequence of):

Sequentially list conditions, if any, leading to the cause listed on line a. Enter the **UNDERLYING CAUSE** (disease or injury that initiated the events resulting in death) **LAST**

b. ____________________

Due to (or as a consequence of):

c. ____________________

Due to (or as a consequence of):

d. ____________________

PART II. Enter other significant conditions contributing to death but not resulting in the underlying cause given in PART I	33. WAS AN AUTOPSY PERFORMED? ☐ Yes ☑ No
	34. WERE AUTOPSY FINDINGS AVAILABLE TO COMPLETE THE CAUSE OF DEATH? ☐ Yes ☐ No

| 36. DID TOBACCO USE CONTRIBUTE TO DEATH?

 ☐   Yes ☐ Probably

 ☑   No ☐ Unknown | 37. IF FEMALE:
 ☐   Not pregnant within past year
 ☐   Pregnant at time of death
 ☐   Not pregnant, but pregnant within 42 days of death
 ☐   Not pregnant, but pregnant 43 days to 1 year before death
 ☐   Unknown if pregnant within the past year | 38. MANNER OF DEATH

 ☐   Natural ☐ Homicide

 ☑   Accident ☐ Pending Investigation

 ☐   Suicide ☐ Could not be determined |

38. DATE OF INJURY (Mo/Day/Yr) (Spell Month) March 4	39. TIME OF INJURY 11:45am	40. PLACE OF INJURY (e.g., Decedent's home; construction site; restaurant; wooded area) Gun range	41. INJURY AT WORK? ☐ Yes ☐ No

42. LOCATION OF INJURY: State: Tortsylvania Street & Number: 5339 Pistol Drive	City or Town: Palsgraf Apartment No.:	Zip Code: 12345

43. DESCRIBE HOW INJURY OCCURRED: Hit by stray bullet discharged by shooting range patron's firearm	44. IF TRANSPORTATION INJURY, SPECIFY: ☐ Driver/Operator ☐ Passenger ☐ Pedestrian ☐ Other (Specify)

45. CERTIFIER (Check only one):
☐   Certifying physician-To the best of my knowledge, death occurred due to the cause(s) and manner stated.
☐   Pronouncing & Certifying physician-To the best of my knowledge, death occurred at the time, date, and place, and due to the cause(s) and manner stated.
☑   Medical Examiner/Coroner-On the basis of examination, and/or investigation, in my opinion, death occurred at the time, date, and place, and due to the cause(s) and manner stated.

Signature of certifier: _____

46. NAME, ADDRESS, AND ZIP CODE OF PERSON COMPLETING CAUSE OF DEATH (Item 32)
Cory Coroner

47. TITLE OF CERTIFIER County Coroner	48. LICENSE NUMBER 68225963C	49. DATE CERTIFIED (Mo/Day/Yr) 06/17/2004	50. FOR REGISTRAR ONLY- DATE FILED (Mo/Day/Yr)

Vaughn Insurance Bureau
500 Main Street
Palsgraf, Tortsylvania

Proof of Income Statement

6/28

To Whom It May Concern:

This letter is to confirm that Damien Ray Dagger was employed by Vaughn Insurance Bureau for the past twelve years.

Last year, Damien Ray Dagger's total income was $102,000 U.S. Dollars.

Two years ago, Damien Ray Dagger's total income was $92,500 U.S. Dollars.

Three years ago, Damien Ray Dagger's total income was $72,480 U.S. Dollars.

Should you have any further questions, please contact me at 800-555-1752 or via email at andre.hr@vaughn.com.

Sincerely,

Andre Alvarez

Director of Human Resources

QUAINT TOWN
ELEMENTARY SCHOOL
123 Primary Dr. Palsgraf, Tortsylvania

Dear Mrs. Dagger,

I hope you are doing well.

I'm sending this note home with Michael to provide context for the journal that is coming home in his backpack. As you know, Michael has been very withdrawn and quiet since your husband's death. I know that Michael and his dad were very close. The other students seem to understand that Michael has lost his dad and that many of them have lost their Little League coach.

Michael does not seem to have any interest in playing during P.E. or recess anymore. He has stopped playing with the other children and spends most of his time disengaged drawing in his journal. When I collected the students' journals today, I saw that Michael's journal is filled with pages and pages of graphic drawings of your husband's death.

I wanted you to be aware of the situation as you support Michael through his grief. Know that the entire school supports Michael, Clara, and your family. You and your husband are pillars of this community and this school.

Please call or email if you would like to discuss this further.

Sincerely,

Tasha Johnson

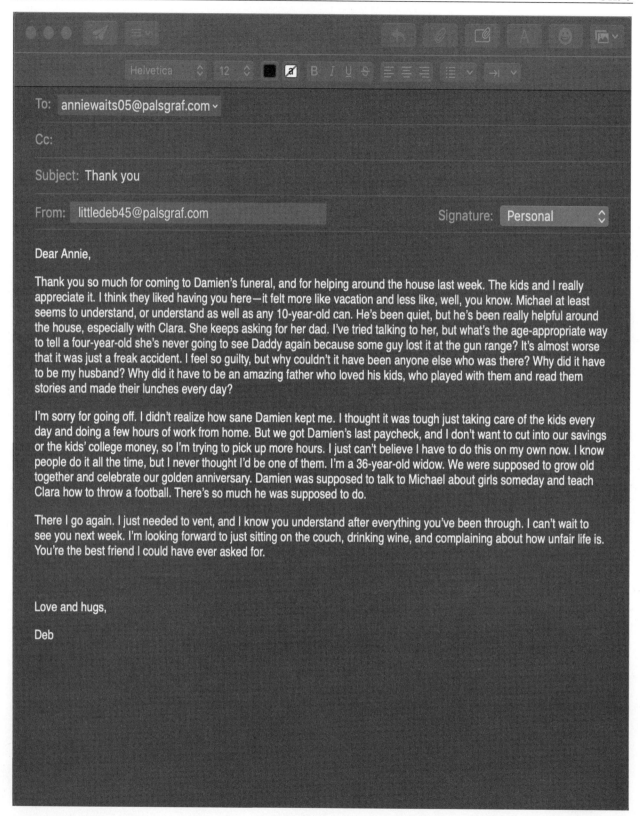

To: anniewaits05@palsgraf.com

Cc:

Subject: Thank you

From: littledeb45@palsgraf.com   Signature: Personal

Dear Annie,

Thank you so much for coming to Damien's funeral, and for helping around the house last week. The kids and I really appreciate it. I think they liked having you here—it felt more like vacation and less like, well, you know. Michael at least seems to understand, or understand as well as any 10-year-old can. He's been quiet, but he's been really helpful around the house, especially with Clara. She keeps asking for her dad. I've tried talking to her, but what's the age-appropriate way to tell a four-year-old she's never going to see Daddy again because some guy lost it at the gun range? It's almost worse that it was just a freak accident. I feel so guilty, but why couldn't it have been anyone else who was there? Why did it have to be my husband? Why did it have to be an amazing father who loved his kids, who played with them and read them stories and made their lunches every day?

I'm sorry for going off. I didn't realize how sane Damien kept me. I thought it was tough just taking care of the kids every day and doing a few hours of work from home. But we got Damien's last paycheck, and I don't want to cut into our savings or the kids' college money, so I'm trying to pick up more hours. I just can't believe I have to do this on my own now. I know people do it all the time, but I never thought I'd be one of them. I'm a 36-year-old widow. We were supposed to grow old together and celebrate our golden anniversary. Damien was supposed to talk to Michael about girls someday and teach Clara how to throw a football. There's so much he was supposed to do.

There I go again. I just needed to vent, and I know you understand after everything you've been through. I can't wait to see you next week. I'm looking forward to just sitting on the couch, drinking wine, and complaining about how unfair life is. You're the best friend I could have ever asked for.

Love and hugs,

Deb

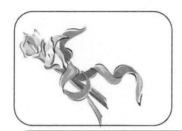

Palsgraf Funeral Home   **INVOICE**

1847 Lily Avenue

Tortsylvania, 12345   INVOICE NO. 5939

DATE   March 6

CLIENT

Debrorah Dagger

36 Sharpe Drive

Tortsylvania, 12345

	QTY	UNIT	ITEM	PRICE	TOTAL
MATERIALS	1	Ea	Mahogany casket	$3500.00	$3500.00
	1	Dz	Flower arrangements	$100.00	$1200.00
	100	Ea	Memorial service programs	$2.00	$200.00

	NAME	SERVICE	FEE	TOTAL
SERVICE		Preparation of the body	$725.00	
		Cosmetics	$250.00	
		Transportation of remains	$325.00	
		Memorial service	$500.00	
		Escort to cemetery	$425.00	
		Use of equipment and staff	$925.00	
		Basic service fee (nonrefundable)	$2100.00	

MATERIALS	$4900.00
SERVICE	$5250.00
TAX	$609.00
TOTAL	$10759.00

III. LEGAL RESEARCH

(A) SUBSTANTIVE LAW

Your legal research reveals that the following statutory provisions apply in the state of Tortsylvania.

411.130 Action for wrongful death—Personal representative to prosecute—Distribution of amount recovered.

(1) Whenever the death of a person results from an injury inflicted by the negligence or wrongful act of another, damages may be recovered for the death from the person who caused it, or whose agent or servant caused it. If the act was willful or the negligence gross, punitive damages may be recovered. The action shall be prosecuted by the personal representative of the deceased.

(2) The amount recovered, less funeral expenses and the cost of administration and costs of recovery including attorney fees, not included in the recovery from the defendant, shall be for the benefit of and go to the kindred of the deceased in the following order:

(a) If the deceased leaves a widow or husband, and no children or their descendants, then the whole to the widow or husband.

(b) If the deceased leaves a widow and children or a husband and children, then one-half (1/2) to the widow or husband and the other one-half (1/2) to the children of the deceased.

(c) If the deceased leaves a child or children, but no widow or husband, then the whole to the child or children.

(d) If the deceased leaves no widow, husband or child, then the recovery shall pass to the mother and father of the deceased, one (1) moiety each, if both are living; if the mother is dead and the father is living, the whole thereof shall pass to the father; and if the father is dead and the mother living, the whole thereof shall go to the mother. In the event the deceased was an adopted person, "mother" and "father" shall mean the adoptive parents of the deceased.

(e) If the deceased leaves no widow, husband or child, and if both father and mother are dead, then the whole of the recovery shall become a part of the personal estate of the deceased, and after the payment of his debts the remainder, if any, shall pass to his kindred more remote than those above named, according to the law of descent and distribution.

411.133 Joinder of wrongful death and personal injury actions.

It shall be lawful for the personal representative of a decedent who was injured by reason of the tortious acts of another, and later dies from such injuries, to recover in the same action for both the wrongful death of the decedent and for the personal injuries from which the decedent suffered prior to death, including a recovery for all elements of damages in both a wrongful death action and a personal injury action.

411.140 What action shall survive.

No right of action for personal injury or for injury to real or personal property shall cease or die with the person injuring or injured, except actions for slander, libel, criminal conversation, and so much of the action for malicious prosecution as is intended to recover for the personal injury. For any other injury an action may be brought or revived by the personal representative, or against the personal representative, heir or devisee, in the same manner as causes of action founded on contract.

(B)   PRACTICE GUIDANCE

Your supervisor has asked you to prepare a settlement demand letter. This is a new task for you as a lawyer. Secondary research sources offer critical explanation and context when you embark on a new lawyering task. Here is an excerpt you located describing the tactical considerations of settlement. You practice in a different state, but the guidance and strategic points are equally applicable to Tortsylvania.

Settlement Tactics in Texas Litigation
by Practical Law Litigation

[Internal Citations Omitted.]

Obtaining a favorable settlement can be a complex process involving many factors, including the case status, the parties' relationship and resources, the strength of the client's claims or defenses and supporting evidence, and state law on issues related to settlement. This Note discusses some of the factors that can help counsel decide whether, when, and how to settle civil litigation proceedings . . . .

Deciding Whether the Client Should Settle

The right to settle a claim belongs exclusively to the client. Counsel may agree to settle a cause of action only if the client gives counsel express authorization to do so.

When advising the client whether to pursue litigation or settlement, counsel must consider many complex issues, not all of which are known when a dispute first arises.

Merits of the Case

In most cases, counsel primarily consider the relative strength of the client's case when discussing settlement recommendations.

When counsel represent a plaintiff in a case where there is clear, convincing evidence that the defendant is subject to liability, they should consider and discuss with the client:

- Their assessment of the client's relatively strong legal position.

- The client's opinion about pursuing litigation.

- The client's possible need to obtain a monetary recovery sooner rather than later.

- The potential benefits in settling the case early based on good facts, to avoid incurring legal fees and other litigation expenses that could cut into a later recovery.

When counsel represent a defendant and the facts strongly suggest that the defendant is subject to liability, they should consider and discuss with the client:

- Their assessment of the client's relatively weak legal position.

- The possibility that an early settlement could mitigate the risk of a larger judgment against the defendant if:

  - the plaintiff strengthens its case during discovery; or

  - the case is pending in a jurisdiction where juries tend to return large verdicts.

- Counsel's assessment of the types of legal fees and expenses that could be avoided by settling earlier in the litigation process.

- The likelihood that settling earlier in the case will minimize the extent of any bad publicity about the client's role in the case.

- The fact that earlier settlement will curtail the type of business disruptions that may be experienced by management and employees who are involved with the litigation proceedings. * * *

Amount at Stake

At the outset of the dispute, counsel should conduct a cost-benefit analysis to consider:

- The potential litigation results.
- The potential settlement outcome.
- The short-term and long-term costs.

It may be worth settling a case if the cost of litigation far exceeds the sum at stake or outweighs the likelihood of success. Counsel should review and update this analysis periodically and when any relevant changes emerge concerning the client's or the opponent's bargaining position.

The Client's Resources

For a client with limited resources, it may be better to attempt to settle early in the case to minimize litigation expense. Alternatively, if the client has extensive resources and the desire to litigate (whether on facts or principle), counsel should factor that into any decision to recommend settlement.

The Opponent's Resources

Counsel representing a plaintiff should obtain information about the defendant's finances and insurance as early as possible, by seeking the information during discovery if necessary. A plaintiff suing a defendant with limited financial resources may find it wiser to pursue settlement earlier in the case, before incurring significant litigation costs (for example, for the expenses of discovery or retaining experts). In most circumstances, counsel should not advise a plaintiff to pursue protracted litigation against a defendant who cannot satisfy any eventual money judgment.

In contrast, a defendant with substantial resources defending claims brought by a plaintiff with limited resources may prefer litigation over settlement. * * *

Additional Litigation Expense

When comparing the cost and likelihood of a plaintiff's recovery by an early settlement against the potential recovery of a favorable future settlement, judgment, or verdict, counsel should take into account both:

- The litigation expenses the plaintiff already incurred.
- The expected additional costs if the plaintiff continues the litigation.

If counsel expect the plaintiff's litigation expenses to escalate as the case proceeds toward trial, a plaintiff may maximize its net recovery by settling for a discounted amount early rather than pursuing a potentially larger future recovery that is diminished by the litigation costs incurred to obtain it.

Similarly, counsel for a defendant should weigh the risks and benefits of an early settlement against those of protracted litigation, considering both the incurred and expected additional litigation costs and the possibility of a future adverse settlement, judgment, or verdict. When counsel expect significant litigation expenses, counsel may suggest that the defendant settle early, which may cost less than continued litigation even if counsel expect the defendant to ultimately prevail.

Counsel for a defendant also should consider whether early settlement or continued litigation in one case may encourage or deter the filing of future cases against that defendant. * * *

Settlement Timing

The timing of a case settlement is a strategic decision. Counsel should evaluate the client's settlement prospects throughout the course of a dispute, taking several factors into account in connection with settlement timing. * * *

Additional Considerations for Achieving a Favorable Settlement

Counsel primarily consider settling to end the dispute. After assessing the party's case and concerns and the issue of settlement timing, counsel should consider other relevant factors to help ensure a favorable settlement for the client. * * *

Relevant Insurance

The client should review its insurance coverage when faced with a claim or potential claim and take all necessary steps to comply with its obligations under the policy and applicable law. For example, an insured party typically must fully and promptly inform its insurance carrier about any claim or potential claim and how the case is developing. An insured party that fails to comply with these types of policy obligations risks that the insurer denies coverage.

Under many policies, the insurer covers an insured party's defense to litigation if the insured gives proper notice of a potentially covered claim. An insured often needs its insurer's advance approval for any settlement before the insurer must cover any part of the settlement. Even absent a policy provision requiring the insurer's consent, if the insured client settles without first notifying the insurer, the client risks having to litigate against its insurer to prove that the claim was covered and the insurer was not prejudiced, which may be difficult to do.

If a party did not provide insurance information in the underlying litigation, counsel should consider whether it benefits the client's position to volunteer the client's insurance information during settlement discussions. Parties are entitled to discover the existence and terms of another party's insurance policy that may be available to satisfy all or part of the judgment or indemnify a liable party. However, counsel should be careful about volunteering the existence or amount of insurance coverage for a claim to avoid implying that the client is prepared to settle up to a certain amount. * * *

Legal Costs

Counsel should consider whether the client's potential expenditures on attorneys' fees and expenses may exceed or significantly offset any potential monetary award. * * *

Nature and Scope of Release

Texas courts will enforce a properly executed release like any other contract. Counsel should carefully consider the nature and scope of any release included in a settlement agreement between the parties.

For the nature of the release, the parties may agree to a release that involves:

- Only one party (typically, the party receiving a settlement payment) granting a release of claims and the other party (typically, the party obligated to make a settlement payment) not granting a release of claims.

- Both parties granting a release of claims and discharging the other party from obligations and liabilities accrued as of the date of the settlement (a mutual release). Including a separate paragraph in the settlement agreement for each party that describes the claims that party agrees to release:

  - allows counsel to tailor the release paragraph to reflect the type of party providing the release (for example, it would not make sense to state that an individual was releasing claims on behalf of her officers and directors); and

- makes it easier for each party to identify what it has agreed to release as compared to the releases that it has been given. * * *

Special Considerations for Multi-Party Disputes

When a dispute involves three or more parties, counsel should weigh several additional considerations.

Related Parties

In cases with multiple parties, counsel should:

- Evaluate each party's potential liability exposure.

- Assess each party's financial resources.

- Consider whether any of the other parties to the dispute are connected to each other in a way that is significant to the dispute.

Parties with a common relationship or whose interests are aligned are more likely to coordinate their strategies and pool their ideas, information, and resources. For example, the defendants may be able to agree on a united defense strategy and avoid falling victim to the plaintiff's "divide and conquer" tactics. If other defendants start settling however, counsel should keep in mind that it is rarely good to be the last defendant remaining in a case. They should reassess the strength of the claims asserted against the client and adjust the client's strategy to account for how any settlements may affect the client's position in the case.

Dividing Liability

When representing a plaintiff, counsel should consider the best approach to obtain the amount desired by the client. Sometimes, a single negotiation with all of the defendants to achieve a collective settlement most efficiently helps counsel obtain the desired amount. In other cases, counsel may prefer to pick one defendant at a time and negotiate an individual settlement before moving on to the next defendant. This approach, commonly known as the "divide and conquer" strategy, effectively puts additional pressure on remaining defendants who otherwise are unwilling to engage in a meaningful settlement dialogue, and sometimes results in a larger total final outcome.

In a tort action not involving strict products liability, where a plaintiff has agreed to a settlement of its claims against fewer than all defendants, releasing one joint tortfeasor:

- Extinguishes the settling party's right to seek contribution from other jointly and severally liable tortfeasors (in most cases).

- Reduces the amount the plaintiff may recover from remaining joint tortfeasors under the "one satisfaction" rule. In a proportional liability case, the sum of all settlement amounts the plaintiff receives from settling defendants for the common injury reduces the amount of damages the plaintiff can recover against the remaining defendants for the same injury.

As a result, a plaintiff who has agreed to settle its claims against fewer than all defendants should ensure that the settlement agreement both specifies the allocation of damages to each cause of action asserted and states how it will reduce any later verdict that the plaintiff may obtain against the remaining co-defendants if the settling defendant is found to be a joint tortfeasor with them.

IV. THE SIMULATION EXERCISE

In this simulation assignment, you will write a settlement demand letter trying to settle survival and wrongful death claims against Harold Husband. Your supervising attorney is growing increasingly concerned about Harold's financial viability. Harold is defending his own criminal case and he is in divorce proceedings. Your supervisor believes that Harold might very well settle to release himself from the claim. Realistically, he would likely settle for the amount of his insurance coverage. This would get some recovery in the hands of the survivors. The plaintiffs would still have claims against the business premise.

A demand letter is a very useful advocacy tool in civil litigation. The goal of a settlement demand letter particularly is to convince the other party to settle the case instead of litigating it in court. Taking a case to trial is costly and time consuming for all parties involved. By laying out your client's case and specifying the damages you are seeking, you give the recipient a chance to end the conflict before discovery or trial.

Imagine what you would want to know as the recipient of such a letter. You have already been sued, so you know the general outline of the case. Here, you would state the specific damages your client is seeking with documentation and support. In Chapter 1, we identified Molly and Damien's intentional torts claims against Harold Husband. At that time, we did not address specifically who would sue on behalf of the deceased or what damages they would be seeking. That is the task presented now in writing a precise and persuasive settlement demand letter.

You are tasked with identifying who has claims against Harold arising from the deaths. You have to read the statute provided to determine who is recovering on behalf of the deceased and what damages are recoverable. Assume you are representing both the estates of Molly and Damien and their qualifying beneficiaries, to the extent they exist. Your demand letter asserts claims for all of these plaintiffs. Leave any other plaintiffs out for this exercise.

The other tricky aspect of wrongful death and survival claims is separating out the damages for each claim. It is helpful to chart all of the claims first, then identify which damage categories are recoverable for each claim. It is often helpful to remember the policy goals of wrongful death (to compensate qualifying beneficiaries who were dependent on the deceased) versus survival (to allow the decedent to recover the claims she would have had if she survived).

For this simulation, assume that the underlying claims are for battery against Harold. Use the practice guidance provided to write persuasively and strategically.

CHAPTER 8

PRODUCTS LIABILITY

I. INTRODUCTION

Products liability is offered as a standalone course in many law schools. First-year torts courses are thus often an introductory survey only of a very complex and sophisticated area of law. It can feel overwhelming for students to absorb a relatively small volume of material across such a relatively large field. Look for big themes as you study the historic pendulum swing between the rights of product manufacturers/sellers and the rights of consumers, ultimately landing somewhere between the two extremes. Look for commonalities in what consumers want the legal framework to be (strict liability) versus what manufacturers/sellers want the legal framework to be (negligence).

On the other hand, this unit is also uniquely relatable to students, which can help balance the challenges of the content's complexity. From Boeing airplanes to Takata airbags to Samsung batteries and hoverboards, students can easily relate to the question of whether a product is reasonably safe for consumers. There is always some gripping current event putting product liability topics in the news to help bring this material to life.

Understanding the history of consumers suing product manufacturers, sellers, and distributors is very helpful to mastering the modern rules. I am reminded of the arcade game "whack-a-mole" in conceptualizing the historic framework. Consumers used to have to match particular claims ranging from express warranty to implied warranty to negligence to strict liability to individual defendants in the supply chain of a particular product. This was tedious and difficult. A purchaser might have an express warranty claim against the manufacturer and a separate implied warranty claim against the seller. A user who was not a purchaser would not have any warranty options and would try to make negligence claims. It would be even more tedious and difficult in modern times given the global business realities of parts manufacturers, distributors, wholesalers, and sellers.

The emergence of strict products liability as a cause of action dramatically transformed the power dynamics between consumers and product manufacturers. It allowed users and consumers to sue any defendant in the supply chain under one single theory asserting that the product was defective. This is a bit of a legal fiction that benefits consumers dramatically. Imagine the shelves and aisles of products at your local Wal-Mart or Target store. Wal-Mart cannot possibly know how the products it sells were designed or manufactured. It just unboxes the shipment of Barbie dolls and Hot Wheels and shelves them. These large chain stores do, however, have their own economic power. If Wal-Mart decides that hoverboards are too dangerous to sell, it can elect to remove them from its shelves before manufacturers have even recalled the product. Wal-Mart can also negotiate an indemnity agreement with manufacturers for any injuries caused by the products it sells.

The modern products liability framework requires consumers to prove that the seller put a product on the market, that it reached the consumer without substantial modification, that the product was in a defective condition, and that the product caused harm. For causes of action like negligence, you might have given approximately equal treatment to each element. For products liability, you will likely spend a disproportionate amount of time analyzing whether a product is defective. The challenge is understanding what exactly makes a product defective.

The Second Restatement of Torts bucketed all products liability claims broadly under the unitary definition of "defective products." Lawyers worked to prove that products were not reasonably safe for consumers. The Third Restatement of Torts broke out the definitions of defective products across three categories: manufacturing defects, design defects, and failure to warn defect theories. These categories are distinct theories to prove a defective product. These categories are often inter-related in pleadings and discovery with multiple theories plead in the alternative. The plaintiff rarely knows exactly why the product malfunctioned until the discovery process.

Consider, for example, when a Duke University basketball player's Nike shoe shreds in an NCAA game causing injury. The plaintiff knows that there is some defect, but what kind exactly? A manufacturing defect is more like finding a product to be what is commonly known as a "lemon" or an anomalous dud. This would mean that the Nike shoe was defective because it did not conform to the manufacturer's own norms. What if, however, the shoe was made exactly right on the assembly line, but it could nonetheless not withstand the rigor of the player's weight, height, or frequency of usage? Perhaps then the shoe is designed defectively for this select category of elite athletes. Or what if there should be instructions governing the proper use of sneakers, suggesting that users should only wear them for so many hours of athletic activity before replacing them? Perhaps then the "defective condition" might be the manufacturer's failure to warn of known risks.

These three approaches to proving a defective product are dramatically different from a lawyering standpoint. Manufacturing defects are often the most straight-forward defect theory to learn and to litigate. It involves a product sample comparator. The case looks at the product that injured the consumer compared to the manufacturer's own specifications for the product. If the product was supposed to be held together by three bolts, but the product that injured the plaintiff was instead held together by only two bolts, that is a manufacturing defect. These defects are more episodic. The costs of compensating for harms caused by the defects can easily be folded into the product pricing.

Design defects are much higher stakes to litigate. They require plaintiffs to show that the product is currently made using X parts, materials, or techniques and instead should have been made using Y parts, materials, or techniques. This defect theory effectively demands a complete redesign of the product line. This is hard to prove and costly to litigate. It is much harder to establish a fixed test or a rule for when a product design is defective. Your textbook materials introduced several competing approaches. For our simulation, we will use the risk-utility factors.

To say that a product is defective because it failed to warn of a risk is the most challenging to conceptualize as a defect. The warnings should be effective for the ordinary consumer. Empower yourself to use your common sense here in thinking through effective warnings. Warnings are not necessary if the dangers are open and obvious (e.g., razors and candles). Product manufacturers must look to what types of uses are foreseeable, even if those uses are not the intended uses. Think, for example, about the new child-proof package designs and warnings not to eat Tide Pods.

The best way to study this material is to spot your own daily use products and pharmaceuticals and study them carefully. Brainstorm what warnings would be appropriate if you were producing the product. You will quickly reveal yourself as a talented drafter of product liability warnings.

Law professors often have to steer students quite heavily and explicitly toward one theory of a defective condition in exam writing. The lawyering challenges get lost in that approach. The reality is that figuring out why a particular product malfunctioned could be a long and costly discovery exercise involving experts, such as engineers and product designers.

In this simulation exercise, you will practice the lawyering skills underlying the field of products liability. Your task is to engage in discovery drafting. You are trying to unravel the mystery of what went wrong with the product. You will need to draft specific questions for the manufacturer defendant to answer. The materials provided reflect the kind of information that a plaintiff's lawyer would be able to access via publicly available sources and her client intake at the outset of discovery. Lawyers then use the discovery process to dig for more information to prove each element of the case. Plaintiff's lawyers need to conduct discovery remembering that they are likely paying these case expenses out of pocket.

This fact pattern involves our Sam Kennedy case file. We met Sam in Chapters 2, 3, and 5. Sam went into the general dentist for a root canal. While the dentist conducted the procedure, a piece of the rotary file equipment broke off into the patient's tooth cavity causing many harms to Sam, such as pain, lost work, and medical bills. The materials provided include some online reviews about the rotary file product, the website materials describing the rotary file, a deposition excerpt, and some legal research on products liability elements. You will draft discovery requests in this simulation exercise.

———————

II. PRODUCT DESCRIPTION

The following text is excerpted from the Rotarious, Inc. website. This is a website selling dental products to consumers (dental practices) directly.

> This rotary file is used in dentistry practices for a variety of purposes. This model is a nickel titanium file used to expose the glide path during a root canal. This state-of-the-art design is perfect for clearing the root canal and determining the working length with extreme precision and efficiency. This model is designed for single use and comes sterile, so there is no need for reprocessing. This file should only be used by a licensed dentist or endodontist.

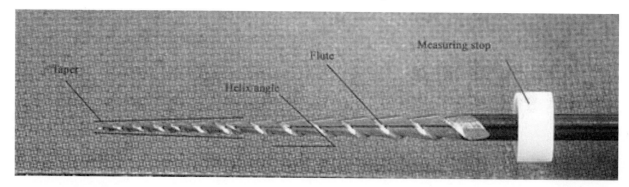

Model R-2000

III. ONLINE PRODUCT REVIEWS

Your online research revealed the following Internet reviews of the product at issue in the case. You previously worked with these same reviews in your Chapter 3 causation simulation.

MODEL R-2000, MANUFACTURED BY ROTARIOUS, INC.

July 3 ★

This feels like it's going to break when even the slightest pressure is applied. I don't like the feel of it. Sorry, not good enough for my dental practice.

January 29 ★ ★

We used one of these files only 4 times and it broke off in the patient's tooth canal. Cheap garbage.

February 1 ★ ★ ★ ★

I got about 6 uses out of these files, not just single use. Better than the last brand I bought.

March 31 ★

Very bad. Flimsy and thin. Do not buy.

April 9 ★ ★ ★ ★

Great product. Light and user-friendly.

May 7 ★ ★ ★

Works great as a single use but wouldn't recommend attempting multiple uses.

August 15 ★ ★ ★

Worked well.

August 17 ★ ★ ★

Worked great. Feels a little weak, but it's so affordable.

IV. DEPOSITION EXCERPT

Below is an excerpt of a deposition of Dr. Taylor Ellington, DMD. Ellington is the defendant in the Sam Kennedy case. This is the relevant excerpt relating to products liability. It excludes all of the formalities and the questions relating to negligence. It focuses only on the narrow question of multiple uses of the dental file.

Q: Doctor, when did you start using the Model R-2000?

A: About two years ago.

Q: And for how long did you use the Model R-2000 in your practice or are you currently still using it?

A: Well, I used it for about a month and then my practice switched back to the old brand I used to use.

Q: Why did you make that change to discontinue use in your dentistry practice?

A: The first time I used a Model R-2000, it was fine. It was like any other file I had used. But I used it a second time and it immediately broke off in the patient's canal. We had to open the canal further in order to get the piece out so we could continue to find our working length.

Q: Was there any injury to the patient because of this?

A: Nothing we couldn't fix. We obviously prefer to open the canal only as much as possible but this time we had to open it further. We were able to fix it with no injury to the patient.

Q: Is that when you stopped using the files?

A: No. I thought it was just a freak thing that the file had malfunctioned, so I used the next one and the same thing happened on its third use.

Q: Was there any harm to the patient the second time the file broke?

A: Yes, there was. We were just about to hit the working length before it broke. The force of it breaking off extended the working length through and into the root. This was concerning because when we perforated the root, we had to take the entire tooth out to avoid infection. We had to give the patient an artificial tooth.

Q: Were there any other incidents in your practice involving the Model R-2000?

A: The third of three incidents was the issue that arose in Sam Kennedy's case that is the subject of this lawsuit.

Q: Yes, I'd like to talk much more about what happened in this case exactly. Before we get to the specifics of Sam's care, when you were using the Model R-2000, how many times were you using the files? Single use? Multiple uses?

A: We generally use the multi-use files about 25 times and the single-use files about 10 times.

Q: Were you aware that the Model R-2000 was labeled as a single-use file?

A: Yes, but no one uses them just once. That's just not how the industry does it. Ask anyone. It's just not economically feasible given their cost and the level of insurance reimbursement coverage that we receive. I've always used these files multiple times and the only time I ever had an issue was with the Model R-2000.

Q: So you reused other comparable models without any issue at all?

A: No other issues with other products. None.

V. LEGAL RESEARCH

(A) SUBSTANTIVE LAW

Your legal research reveals the following statutory provisions adopting portions of the Second and Third Restatement of Torts provisions on strict products liability in Tortsylvania.

(1) Restatement Provisions

§ 402A. Special Liability of Seller of Product for
Physical Harm to User or Consumer
(Second Restatement of Torts)

(1) One who sells any product in a defective condition unreasonably dangerous to the user or consumer or to his property is subject to liability for physical harm thereby caused to the ultimate user or consumer, or to his property, if

(a) the seller is engaged in the business of selling such a product, and

(b) it is expected to and does reach the user or consumer without substantial change in the condition in which it is sold.

(2) The rule stated in Subsection (1) applies although

(a) the seller has exercised all possible care in the preparation and sale of his product, and

(b) the user or consumer has not bought the product from or entered into any contractual relation with the seller.

§ 2. Categories of Product Defect
(Third Restatement of Torts) (emphasis added)

A product is defective when, at the time of sale or distribution it contains a manufacturing defect, is defective in design, or is defective because of inadequate warning or instructions. A product:

- Contains a <u>manufacturing defect</u> when the product departs from its intended design even though all possible care was exercised in the preparation and marketing of the product;

- Is <u>defective in design</u> when the foreseeable risks of harm posed by the product could have been reduced or avoided by the adoption of a reasonable alternative design by the seller or other distributor, or a predecessor in the commercial chain of distribution, and the omission of the alternative design renders the product not reasonably safe;

- Is defective because of <u>inadequate instructions or warnings</u> when the foreseeable risks of harm posed by the product could have been reduced or avoided by the provision of reasonable instructions or warnings by the seller or other distributor, or a predecessor in the commercial chain of distribution, and the omission of the instructions or warnings renders the product not reasonably safe.

(2) Risk Utility Factors

In this jurisdiction, the risk utility factors are used when determining if there is a design defect. The court looks at the factors as a whole to decide if the risk outweighs the utility.

Risk Utility Analysis Factors
44 Miss. L.J. 825 (1973)
On the Nature of Strict Tort Liability for Products
John W. Wade

- The usefulness and desirability of the product—its utility to the user and to the public as a whole.

- The safety aspects of the product—the likelihood that it will cause injury, and the probable seriousness of the injury.

- The availability of a substitute product which would meet the same need and not be as unsafe.

- The manufacturer's ability to eliminate the unsafe character of the product without impairing its usefulness or making it too expensive to maintain its utility.

- The user's ability to avoid danger by the exercise of care in the use of the product.

- The user's anticipated awareness of the dangers inherent in the product and their avoidability, because of the general public knowledge of the obvious condition of the product, or of the existence of suitable warnings or instructions.

- The feasibility, on the part of the manufacturer, of spreading the loss by setting the price of the product or carrying liability insurance.

(B) PROCEDURAL RULES

Your legal research reveals the following procedural rules governing interrogatories. These rules come from the Federal Rules of Civil Procedure. Federal rules would apply in federal court. In civil procedure you will study whether a claim is brought in federal or state court. Many tort law cases will be state cases applying state rules of procedure. The federal rules are used for this simulation because it likely reinforces your civil procedure course content.

Rule 33—Interrogatories to Parties

(a) **In General.**

(1) *Number.* Unless otherwise stipulated or ordered by the court, a party may serve on any other party no more than 25 written interrogatories, including all discrete subparts. Leave to serve additional interrogatories may be granted to the extent consistent with Rule 26(b)(1) and (2).

(2) *Scope.* An interrogatory may relate to any matter that may be inquired into under Rule 26(b). An interrogatory is not objectionable merely because it asks for an opinion or contention that relates to fact or the application of law to fact, but the court may order that the interrogatory need not be answered until designated discovery is complete, or until a pretrial conference or some other time.

VI.   THE SIMULATION EXERCISE

Using the materials provided, you will represent the plaintiff, Sam Kennedy, in asking questions of the product manufacturer to discover whether Sam's injury was caused by a manufacturing defect, a design defect, a failure to warn defect, or no defect at all. You will draft interrogatories to be sent to the product manufacturer to obtain information about the product.

Your goal in writing these interrogatories is to understand what went wrong for your client. Was this particular file just a "lemon" that malfunctioned in a freak incident that failed to conform with the manufacturer's own standards? That would reflect a manufacturing defect. What questions might you ask to ferret this defect out? Are all of the files that the manufacturer produced defective because of the way that they are designed, such as the materials used? This would reflect a design defect. What warnings were provided with this product? Were they effective? You are trying to uncover information that will prove your legal theory that the product was designed defectively.

Interrogatories are a lesson in careful drafting. Your inquires need to be specific enough that the defendant can understand your question and answer it clearly. You do not want interrogatories to be too broad because they will yield an objection that they are too broad or too burdensome. You do not want them to be too narrow because they will not yield enough productive information. Below are some sample interrogatories that might help stimulate your thinking. Think about this like your construction of a "wish list" of all of the information and documents that you would like to obtain to understand what happened to your client and how this product may have caused it.

In a separate section of the Interrogatories, the terms used would be defined specifically and clearly. There are also some typical preliminary questions, such as a question about who at the company helped prepare these responses. For now, just focus on your initial efforts to draft the substantive interrogatories that get at the heart of your "defective condition" element. Your professor will provide more details on how many and what format to follow. Below are some sample interrogatories:

SAMPLE INTERROGATORIES

SAMPLE INTERROGATORY NO. 1: Please identify the person or person(s) who participated in any manner in the design and engineering of the Model R-2000 rotary dental file. For each person identified, please provide the person's name, address, telephone number, job title, job responsibilities, dates of employment, and if they are no longer employed, the date and reason for termination.

ANSWER:

[*TIP: Note how incredibly specific and detailed this request is. You do not want just a list of names sent back to you. You are limited in how many "asks" you get, so there is a lot of information packed in this one interrogatory. You want to know if the identified individuals are still at the company and how to get in touch with them if you want to depose them.*]

SAMPLE INTERROGATORY NO. 2: Please identify each Model R-2000 complaint or adverse event report that Rotarious, Inc. has received, including the date received and the consumer who submitted the Complaint.

ANSWER:

SAMPLE INTERROGATORY NO. 3: Identify the specific provision(s) of each governmental or industry regulation, standard, guideline, recommendation, accepted practice, or custom that you contend was applicable to the design, manufacture, performance, or testing of the product.

ANSWER:

SAMPLE INTERROGATORY NO. 4: If there was a change after the date of manufacture of The Product in the manufacturing process of the component(s) at issue (or component substantially similar to the component(s) at issue):

    (a)   state the nature of the change;

    (b)   state the reason for the change;

    (c)   state the date of the change;

    (d)   identify each person who directed the change; and

    (e)   identify each document that implements the change.

ANSWER:

CHAPTER 9

DEFENSES

I. INTRODUCTION

Defenses are a dynamic unit to develop savvy lawyering skills. This chapter is a chance to see how the plaintiff's case and the defendant's case meet in an adversarial context. It is also a chance to intersect substantive tort law with civil procedure. This simulation is an important tool to see defenses in action and to understand their importance to the architecture of a lawsuit.

Sequencing is important here. Defenses, by definition, defend against an initial cause of action. The plaintiff will sue the defendant for a particular cause of action first. The civil complaint initiates the lawsuit, identifies the cause(s) of action, and pleads facts sufficient to support the claim(s). You practiced drafting a complaint in Chapter 1, for example. The defendant then receives the complaint, reviews the allegations, and decides how to respond. The defendant can respond by denying the allegations and/or the defendant can raise its own defenses. Some defenses must be raised or they are waived. These pleading and answer rules are the subject of your civil procedure studies.

Defenses are notably different from counter arguments in the pleading requirements. Defenses are generally counter claims that need to be plead affirmatively by the defendant in an answer or they are waived. The burden of proof is on the defendant to prove the defense. There are defenses that are common law defenses and others that are statutory defenses. This simulation uses a statutory defense because statutory analysis and interpretation are critical skills often neglected in the first-year case method of study.

There are several defenses that you will study in your primary casebook, including contributory and comparative negligence, express and implied waivers, statutes of limitations, and immunities. In this simulation, you will focus narrowly on a defense to an intentional tort of battery. The simulation learning objectives translate to each of these defenses though. Lawyering defenses requires you to issue-spot claims accurately and thoroughly, plead claims with sufficient facts, and think strategically about the hierarchy of defenses.

Just as we considered pleading in the alternative in Chapter 1 as we identified our intentional torts claims, so too do we have to consider pleading defenses in the alternative. If the defendant has multiple defenses to plead, might one defense be a complete bar on recovery relative to other defenses that might only be partial defenses?

This chapter reprints the Sharp Shooter's Gun Range police report for your ease and convenience in brainstorming defenses. In Chapter 1, you focused primarily on suing Harold as the defendant. You might also have issue-spotted that Harold suffered injuries from Will too. You will narrowly focus on a battery suit of Harold v. Will in this simulation exercise. You will review relevant statutes providing self-defense and defense of others rules. You may also use any cases or doctrine from your casebook. You will be brainstorming the defenses that Will would plead in an answer against a battery complaint by Harold Husband.

II. POLICE REPORT

Case No: 294850-398494   **Date:** March 4

Reporting Officer: Officer Clayton Brown   **Prepared By:** Officer Clayton Brown

Incident: Shooting accident at Sharp Shooter's Gun Range, killing a male patron on impact, injuring a female patron—ultimately leading to her death days later, and injuring two more patrons.

Detail of Event:

On March 4, Harold Husband went to the Sharp Shooter's Gun Range at approximately 11 a.m. to engage in target shooting. While at the range, he received a text message from his wife, Wendy, at 11:43 a.m. stating, "I know you R @ the range. Sorry to do this by text, I knew you would lose it when I told you. I'm divorcing U." Ervin Employee said he heard Harold Husband start crying and muttering things like "I cannot go on without her" and "how could she do this." Ervin Employee then saw Harold Husband take his gun and fire it repeatedly in the air, not directly at any patrons.

One of the shots hit Damien Dagger, a patron at Sharp Shooter's, in the head and killed him on impact. Another shot hit Molly May in the left side of her chest. Gertrude Guest and Ervin Employee hid behind the wooden barrier between Harold's lane and the lane Gertrude was in. Two of the bullets pierced the wooden barrier between lanes, injuring Gertrude Guest in the arm and Ervin Employee in the leg. Will Witness jumped on the back of Harold Husband after a few shots were fired, restraining him until the police arrived.

Actions Taken:

When I arrived at the scene, I ran to Harold Husband and removed the gun. He complained of severe pain in his shoulder and was escorted in an ambulance to the hospital with Officer Hobbes. I observed the deceased body of Damien Dagger. Molly May was taken to the hospital in the first ambulance, as she was non-responsive. Ervin Employee and Gertrude Guest were taken in the ambulances that arrived later.

I recovered the phone of Harold Husband in his lane, along with the semi-automatic weapon involved in the accident. He had rented this weapon from the facility. There was also a bag belonging to Harold Husband containing his wallet.

There were marks on the ceiling of the gun range, and holes in the wooden partitions separating lanes on both the right and left sides. Broken glass from lights that had been shattered was also on the ground.

Will Witness was uninjured. He stated that while shooting he saw a light shatter and heard people screaming. He located where Harold was shooting wildly in the air and brought him down to the ground.

I then went to the hospital to interview witnesses. Molly May was in critical condition. Ervin Employee required 12 stitches in the leg. Gertrude Guest required surgery for a shattered bone in her arm. Harold Husband had a separated shoulder from contact with Will Witness. [Upon later investigation, Molly May died two days later from an infection in her gunshot wound. Gertrude Guest is in therapy for post-traumatic stress disorder and night terrors.]

III. LEGAL RESEARCH

(A) SUBSTANTIVE LAW

Your research uncovers the following legal authorities that govern in Tortsylvania. This law is actually excerpted from the Arizona Code. Assume for this exercise that it applies in our jurisdiction.

§ 13–404. Justification; self-defense

A. Except as provided in subsection B of this section, a person is justified in threatening or using physical force against another when and to the extent a reasonable person would believe that physical force is immediately necessary to protect himself against the other's use or attempted use of unlawful physical force.

B. The threat or use of physical force against another is not justified:

1. In response to verbal provocation alone; or

2. To resist an arrest that the person knows or should know is being made by a peace officer or by a person acting in a peace officer's presence and at his direction, whether the arrest is lawful or unlawful, unless the physical force used by the peace officer exceeds that allowed by law; or

3. If the person provoked the other's use or attempted use of unlawful physical force, unless:

(a) The person withdraws from the encounter or clearly communicates to the other his intent to do so reasonably believing he cannot safely withdraw from the encounter; and

(b) The other nevertheless continues or attempts to use unlawful physical force against the person.

§ 13–406. Justification; defense of a third person

A person is justified in threatening or using physical force or deadly physical force against another to protect a third person if, under the circumstances as a reasonable person would believe them to be, such person would be justified under section 13–404 . . . in threatening or using physical force or deadly physical force to protect himself against the unlawful physical force or deadly physical force a reasonable person would believe is threatening the third person he seeks to protect.

(B) PROCEDURAL RULES

Below are excerpts from the Federal Rules of Civil Procedure. Rule 8 advises you how to style a response to a complaint for civil relief. Rule 8(a) helped you write your complaint in Chapter 1. The rest of Rule 8 informs your lawyering here.

These are federal rules that would apply in federal court. In civil procedure you will study whether a claim is brought in federal or state court. Many tort law cases will be state cases applying state rules of procedure. The federal rules are used for this simulation because it likely reinforces your civil procedure course content.

Rule 8. General Rules of Pleading

* * * (b) Defenses; Admissions and Denials.

    (1) In General. In responding to a pleading, a party must:

        (A) state in short and plain terms its defenses to each claim asserted against it; and

(B) admit or deny the allegations asserted against it by an opposing party.

(2) Denials—Responding to the Substance. A denial must fairly respond to the substance of the allegation.

(3) General and Specific Denials. A party that intends in good faith to deny all the allegations of a pleading—including the jurisdictional grounds—may do so by a general denial. A party that does not intend to deny all the allegations must either specifically deny designated allegations or generally deny all except those specifically admitted.

(4) Denying Part of an Allegation. A party that intends in good faith to deny only part of an allegation must admit the part that is true and deny the rest.

(5) Lacking Knowledge or Information. A party that lacks knowledge or information sufficient to form a belief about the truth of an allegation must so state, and the statement has the effect of a denial.

(6) Effect of Failing to Deny. An allegation—other than one relating to the amount of damages—is admitted if a responsive pleading is required and the allegation is not denied. If a responsive pleading is not required, an allegation is considered denied or avoided.

(c) Affirmative Defenses.

(1) In General. In responding to a pleading, a party must affirmatively state any avoidance or affirmative defense, including:

- accord and satisfaction;
- arbitration and award;
- assumption of risk;
- contributory negligence;
- duress;
- estoppel;
- failure of consideration;
- fraud;
- illegality;
- injury by fellow servant;
- laches;
- license;
- payment;
- release;
- res judicata;
- statute of frauds;
- statute of limitations; and
- waiver. * * *

(d) Pleading to Be Concise and Direct; Alternative Statements; Inconsistency.

(1) In General. Each allegation must be simple, concise, and direct. No technical form is required.

(2) Alternative Statements of a Claim or Defense. A party may set out 2 or more statements of a claim or defense alternatively or hypothetically, either in a single count or defense or in separate ones. If a party makes alternative statements, the pleading is sufficient if any one of them is sufficient.

(3) Inconsistent Claims or Defenses. A party may state as many separate claims or defenses as it has, regardless of consistency. * * *

(C) PRACTICE GUIDANCE

You have never written an answer before as a new attorney. You thus take some time to research practitioner materials that might guide you, provide templates, and save valuable time and resources. In your research, you locate a sample answer template raising an affirmative defense of self-defense. It is excerpted here. This is a template of general use to practitioners. Savvy lawyers would use a template as a starting point, but then they would modify, tweak, and adapt the form to their precise governing law and facts.

2A American Jurisprudence Pleading & Practice Forms Assault and Battery § 177 (March 2020)

§ 177. Answer—Force used necessary for self-protection—Force used to prevent battery by plaintiff

ANSWER

Defendant, *[name of defendant]*, in answer to the complaint filed in the above-entitled matter, admits, denies, and alleges as follows:

1. Defendant denies the allegations contained in *[Paragraph/Paragraphs] [[number of paragraph]/[numbers of paragraphs]]* of the complaint.

2. Defendant denies on information and belief the allegations contained in *[Paragraph/ Paragraphs] [[number of paragraph]/[numbers of paragraphs]]* of the complaint.

3. Defendant lacks sufficient information or belief to admit or deny the allegations contained in *[Paragraph/Paragraphs] [[number of paragraph]/[numbers of paragraphs]]* of the complaint and denies those allegations on that ground.

4. In answer to Paragraph *[number of paragraph]* of the complaint, defendant admits that *[description of allegation admitted]*, and denies all of the remaining allegations contained in that paragraph.

5. In answer to Paragraph *[number of paragraph]* of the complaint, defendant denies on information and belief that *[description of allegation denied on information and belief]*, and denies all of the remaining allegations contained in that paragraph.

6. In answer to Paragraph *[number of paragraph]* of the complaint, defendant lacks sufficient information or belief to admit or deny that *[description of allegation as to which defendant lacks sufficient information or belief to admit or deny]*, and denies that allegation on that ground. Defendant denies all of the remaining allegations contained in Paragraph *[number of paragraph]*.

7. Further answering the complaint, defendant alleges that at the time mentioned in plaintiff's complaint, and immediately prior to the time when defendant is alleged to have committed the acts described in plaintiff's complaint, plaintiff willfully, wrongfully, and unlawfully made an assault on defendant, and would have beaten, bruised, and struck defendant if defendant had not immediately defended *[himself/herself]*. As a result of the conduct of plaintiff, defendant defended *[himself/herself]* and in so doing necessarily and

unavoidably beat, bruised, and struck plaintiff, but only to the extent necessary for defendant's own defense and to prevent plaintiff from committing a battery on defendant.

8. Any damage or injury suffered by plaintiff was occasioned by plaintiff's own wrongful acts.

9. The conduct of defendant as described above is the same conduct alleged in plaintiff's complaint as the basis for defendant's liability.

WHEREFORE, defendant requests judgment by the court:

1. Ordering that plaintiff take nothing by the complaint filed in the above-entitled matter, and that the same be dismissed with prejudice;

2. Awarding defendant costs; and

3. Granting defendant such other and further relief as the court deems just and proper.

Dated: *[date of answer]*

———————————

[Name of attorney for defendant]

IV. THE SIMULATION EXERCISE

You are representing Will Witness, who is being sued by Harold Husband for civil battery. Above is a copy of Officer Brown's police report, in which he discusses how Will stopped Harold from continuing to discharge his firearm after injuring several people at the range. In addition, you have the applicable state statutes governing self-defense and defense of others.

Brainstorm the affirmative defenses you could plead on your client's behalf. Which defenses are the strongest? How would you apply the elements of self-defense and defense of others to your client's actions? What facts are you likely to admit? What facts would you deny, if any?

Draft an answer building off of the template provided. Customize the template for the statutes and facts provided.

CHAPTER 10

JOINT TORTFEASORS

I. INTRODUCTION

This chapter contains some of the higher order concepts of the torts course. It asks, what happens when we have multiple defendants who each contributed to the plaintiff's harm? Does the plaintiff pursue multiple suits in a piecemeal approach against each individual defendant, cobbling together partial recoveries to make the plaintiff whole? Does the plaintiff select one defendant who is the most financially viable and seek full recovery from that defendant? Does it matter which tort or damage category is at issue? These are all complex and technical inquiries that reflect an intersection between substantive tort law, civil procedure, and the strategic realities of financial viability and relationships.

This unit can be understood by framing the topic in four parts—the types of joint tortfeasors, the jurisdictional split, the procedural premise, and the lawyering implications. This unit sits entirely on the defendant side of the litigation "v." It is about how damages are apportioned among defendants. It has nothing to do with the plaintiff's relative fault.

First, a brief review of the types of joint tortfeasors. Joint tortfeasors are a subset of co-defendants. Not all co-defendants are joint tortfeasors. Co-defendants can become joint tortfeasors because they share a common duty to the plaintiff, because they each acted separately to create the plaintiff's indivisible injury, or because they acted in concert. Your textbook introduced each of these categories. This chapter brings these concepts to life in a lawyering context.

Second, this is a very impactful jurisdictional split to master. Visually, it is helpful to consider the joint tortfeasor issue as one large pie sharing exercise considering how the "liability pie" will be sliced up among joint tortfeasor defendants to compensate the plaintiff. You will study one major jurisdictional split between several liability jurisdictions and joint and several liability jurisdictions. There are numerous deviations and hybrids as well of these two main rules.

Several liability jurisdictions only allow each defendant to be liable for their allocated share of the harm. If D1 is 20% liable, D2 is 60% liable, and D3 is 20% liable, even if D3 is unavailable for suit, D1 and D2 will never pay more than their shares of 20% and 60%, respectively. In this scenario, the plaintiff bears the cost of D3's absence and can only be made 80% whole under the best of circumstances.

In joint and several liability jurisdictions, if the defendants qualify as joint tortfeasors, then one of the tortfeasors could be sued for the plaintiff's entire recovery. The practical implications of this joint and several liability framework are quite significant. If a large financially viable corporate defendant is one of the defendants, a plaintiff can efficiently recoup 100% of the recovery from that defendant solely.

This, in turn, triggers rights of contribution. In a contribution action, the viable defendant that overpaid its allocated share to the plaintiff can now seek recovery from the other defendants. The joint tortfeasors now owe the defendant directly instead of the plaintiff.

With the definitions and jurisdictions solidified, the procedural premise now comes into better focus. The premise of joint tortfeasor issues actually begins at the intersection of torts and civil procedure. The civil procedure rule of permissive joinder allows plaintiffs to elect whether to sue all or some of the defendants in any one lawsuit. This strategic procedural decision is most often informed by relationships to defendants, the availability of defendants to be sued, and the financial viability of defendants. This procedural premise sets up interesting strategic considerations of lawyering in a joint tortfeasor scenario.

Transitioning to the strategic implications of joint tortfeasor liability, imagine that a passenger in a car accident suffers an injury. The driver of the passenger's car (D1) was speeding and could not control the vehicle. The driver hit a Wal-Mart truck (D2) that had also swerved into D1's lane because the Wal-Mart truck driver (D3) was texting and driving.

First, we need to identify and define a joint tortfeasor relationship. D1 and D2 are joint tortfeasors because their separate acts of negligence (speeding and texting, respectively) combined to create the plaintiff's indivisible injury. There might be a third joint tortfeasor if the plaintiff wanted to sue the individual truck driver (the employee) in addition to Wal-Mart (the employer). D2 and D3 would be joint tortfeasors because they share a common duty to the plaintiff.

For strategic financial reasons, in joint and several liability jurisdictions, the passenger might elect to sue only Wal-Mart (D2) believing that Wal-Mart can make the passenger whole most efficiently. The plaintiff might elect not to sue D3 because the added costs and logistics are unnecessary. The decision to pursue D2 might also be informed by relationships. The fact that the passenger was riding with D1 suggests that they have some relationship. D2 might not want to sue D1 because of that relationship or because of the relative financial viability.

In joint and several liability jurisdictions, this leaves D2 overpaying more than its share of the liability because of the procedural premise that allowed the plaintiff to elect only one defendant and the substantive rule that made D2 liable for the full harm as a joint tortfeasor.

Contribution is the solution that might allow D2 to remedy the wrong of overpaying. D2 can pursue its own suit against D1 and/or D3 in contribution to be made whole for the absent defendants' share of the liability. This can happen in the same suit by impleading D1 and/or D3 or in a separate suit. This still positions D2 to bear the costs of being made whole and allows the plaintiff to be made whole more efficiently.

In several liability jurisdictions, the plaintiff can still elect to only sue D2, but the plaintiff will then only recover D2's allocated share of the liability. If the plaintiff wants to be made fully whole, D1 must also be joined to the suit by the plaintiff. In this scenario, contribution has no significance because D2 cannot overpay D1's share.

It is still significant to D2, however, that D1 is not in the case. If we return to thinking of this activity as dividing up the pie among defendants, D2's legal strategy can now seek to drive up the jury's allocation to D1 as a strategy to reduce D2's fault. Thus, while the plaintiff may elect not to sue D1 in several liability jurisdictions too, this procedural choice will reduce plaintiff's overall recovery. D2 will not pick up D1's share. D2 can even try to reduce its liability by strategically arguing that the absent defendant holds a great share of the liability.

Recall that not all co-defendants are joint tortfeasors. Imagine, for example, if the passenger in the car accident contracted the COVID-19 virus at the hospital due to improper cleaning and isolation practices. The hospital's liability would not factor into the joint tortfeasor analysis because the hospital is a successive tortfeasor (not concurrent) and because the harm is divisible.

This chapter is an important moment to highlight the role of statutory law in torts. We spend most of the course looking predominantly at common law cases to discern governing rules, which can distort the reality that many statutes govern the field as well. You will extract rules from sample statutes in this exercise. You will practice reading statutes precisely and carefully.

Client counseling, civil procedure, and statutory analysis are all critical tools to mastering the joint tortfeasors material. You will practice each of these skills in this simulation. This simulation builds on the Kennedy dental malpractice case file. The Kennedy case file identified the dental file manufacturer as another possible defendant because the file broke off in Kennedy's mouth. This might create a products liability suit for the same indivisible injuries as the dental malpractice suit. The products liability theory was explored in Chapter 8. In the following materials, you will combine the procedural premise with statutory rules on joint tortfeasors to advise your client strategically.

————————

II. CLIENT E-MAIL

Date: March 31, 2:18 p.m.

RE: Who we sue in my case

Hi,

Thanks for working on my behalf. I am a bit uncomfortable with the idea of suing Dr. Ellington. I would like to discuss this with you further to understand my options. My mother told me that she and my dad have spent a lot of time with Dr. Ellington over the years. My parents are so disappointed with me for dragging Dr. Ellington into court because the Ellingtons are family friends and pillars of our tightknit community.

It seems like the dental instrument breaking was a huge part of what happened to me. While Dr. Ellington is not blameless, is it possible to focus on suing only the manufacturer who made the file rather than the dentist for now? Could we just see how that suit goes first? What would that process look like? Would it limit how much money I can recover?

Please let me know what my options are.

Thank you,

Sam

III. LEGAL RESEARCH

For this assignment, we will study how different statutes yield different outcomes. Below are two separate statutes that your research might yield depending on your jurisdiction. One is from a joint and several liability jurisdiction. One is from a several liability jurisdiction. Label them accurately first.

JURISDICTION 1 STATUTE

A judgment against one of several joint wrongdoers shall not bar the prosecution of an action against any or all the others, but the injured party may bring separate actions against the wrongdoers and proceed to judgment in each, or, if sued jointly, he may proceed to judgment against them successively until judgment has been rendered against, or the cause has been otherwise disposed of as to, all of the defendants, and no bar shall arise as to any of them by reason of a judgment against another, or others, until the judgment has been satisfied. If there be a judgment against one or more joint wrongdoers, the full satisfaction of such judgment accepted as such by the plaintiff shall be a discharge of all joint wrongdoers, except as to the costs; provided, however, this section shall have no effect on the right of contribution between joint wrongdoers.

JURISDICTION 2 STATUTE

(1) In all tort actions, including products liability actions, involving fault of more than one (1) party to the action, including third-party defendants and persons who have been released under subsection (4) of this section, the court, unless otherwise agreed by all parties, shall instruct the jury to answer interrogatories or, if there is no jury, shall make findings indicating:

   (a)   The amount of damages each claimant would be entitled to recover if contributory fault is disregarded; and

   (b)   The percentage of the total fault of all the parties to each claim that is allocated to each claimant, defendant, third-party defendant, and person who has been released from liability under subsection (4) of this subsection.

(2) In determining the percentages of fault, the trier of fact shall consider both the nature of the conduct of each party at fault and the extent of the causal relation between the conduct and the damages claimed.

(3) The court shall determine the award of damages to each claimant in accordance with the findings, subject to any reduction under subsection (4) of this section, and shall determine and state in the judgment each party's equitable share of the obligation to each claimant in accordance with the respective percentages of fault.

(4) A release, covenant not to sue, or similar agreement entered into by a claimant and a person liable, shall discharge that person from all liability for contribution, but it shall not be considered to discharge any other persons liable upon the same claim unless it so provides. However, the claim of the releasing person against other persons shall be reduced by the amount of the released persons' equitable share of the obligation, determined in accordance with the provisions of this section.

IV. THE SIMULATION EXERCISE

For this simulation exercise, your client is Sam Kennedy. Sam has sent you the preceding email. Sam is conflicted about bringing a lawsuit against the dentist, Dr. Ellington, because of family relationships. Your client wants to know the implications of possibly pursuing only the product manufacturer.

One version of this assignment will require you to draft two separate emails to your client reflecting the jurisdictional split between the two statutes located in your legal research. Alternatively, your professor may divide your class in half and have each group draft one email. In practice, you would only be sending one of these messages because your statutory research would reveal either a rule like statute 1 or like statute 2 (or a variation of them). This simulation uses both jurisdictions, in the alternative, to practice client counseling and to master strategic lawyering concepts. Your email(s) should explain the options and consequences of seeking recovery solely from the product manufacturer. Simply stated, if Sam only sued the product manufacturer, could Sam be made 100% whole or only partially compensated?

This is an opportunity to practice defining technical legal concepts in a manner that your client will understand. It is also an exercise in providing clear legal advice. Often times our law school classrooms sit so heavily in the "maybe." Many real-world client questions have far more concrete answers than that. Our clients demand as much clarity and certainty as we can realistically provide. Explain your reasoning to the client clearly with proper professionalism and tone.

CHAPTER 11

STRICT LIABILITY

I. INTRODUCTION

Strict liability is a unique cause of action in tort law. Strict liability exists because there are some activities that are just too dangerous to be done safely, no matter how careful the defendant is. If strict liability applies, the plaintiff will recover for harms resulting from that activity. It is an "if→ then" analysis when it applies. It is therefore rare when applied because its effects are so sweeping.

Notably, many of the leading tort law casebooks present cases for discussion in which strict liability claims fail as a matter of law. It can be tricky for students to learn an entire field of law by studying cases that do not find liability. Consider why that is so. If strict liability is largely an if→then analysis, once you know a particular activity is subject to strict liability in your jurisdiction, blasting for example, then the case would likely settle or never be filed at all. There will only be narrow and limited defenses left for the defendant to assert. Plaintiffs might recover by simply demonstrating their harms to the defendant and receiving compensation with relative ease.

The central focus in strict liability analysis is thus on whether an activity is subject to strict liability at all. Each jurisdiction uses a term of art to define what qualifies. Most jurisdictions require that the activity be "abnormally dangerous." Others look to whether it is "ultra-hazardous" or other similar terms.

The task of determining whether an activity is abnormally dangerous is a large "apples to apples" exercise in which lawyers try to consider whether a new activity is more like existing activities that courts have previously held to be abnormally dangerous or whether it is more like cases that do not fall under existing strict liability rules, but rather are analyzed through an ordinary negligence lens.

Blasting is the iconic example of an abnormally dangerous activity. Applying a simple "apples to apples" test comparing activities like driving, operating farm machinery, or playing sports to blasting reveals that these activities can be done far safer than blasting. Ordinary due care negligence principles are enough to manage the risks of harm in most activities. The strict liability test applies the Restatement factors to the activity in the community in which it occurred. Activities that might be abnormally dangerous in an urban location might not be in a rural setting.

Students should be careful to identify only activities that might be subject to strict liability, not products or conditions on land. Activities are actions like blasting, transporting hazardous chemicals, and spraying pesticides. In contrast, the buildings, chemicals, and pesticides themselves are products or conditions that trigger different liability lenses in tort law.

Remember that courts are analyzing the abnormally dangerous activity as an activity in its entirety, not the injuries that triggered the case. Fight the instinct to frame the test through a consequentialist lens looking at the activity only when it did cause harm. A consequentialist lens mistakenly embeds the harm that did occur in the very definition of the activity, thus writing the strict liability question out of the case entirely. For example, if the question is framed as whether it is abnormally dangerous to operate a firing range that rented an Uzi to a child who, unable to control the machinery, inadvertently shot her instructor, it only leads to a "yes" in that instance. The strict liability question is whether it is *always* abnormally dangerous to operate a firing range, not the narrower facts in which harm did already occur at the firing range.

Strict liability analysis considers whether the activity can be done safely when done non-negligently. Accidents can surely happen at gun ranges, but the question is, if everything is working correctly and non-negligently, is the activity abnormally dangerous where it is occurring? That is why blasting stands out so clearly. No matter how many signs are posted, trainings are conducted, and protocols are followed, the uncertainty of blasting creates risk of harm no matter how reasonably it is done.

Finally, two procedural reminders before beginning this assigned simulation. (1) Remember that strict liability involves pleading in the alternative. As lawyers make their arguments whether strict liability applies, if the answer is "no," the claim might still be viable under a negligence cause of action or alternative theory. (2) The question of whether an activity is abnormally dangerous is decided as a matter of law, not as a factual matter put before the jury.

This simulation exercise is contained in this chapter only. It does not build on the Kennedy or Sharp Shooter's fact patterns used throughout prior chapters. If you think about the points just introduced in this section, you will see why. Framing a strict liability client simulation has to challenge an entire industry as abnormally dangerous. Sure, accidents do happen in dental care and in the operation of shooting ranges, but ordinary negligence principles are enough to manage those risks. A strict liability simulation necessarily has to challenge an entire activity.

In this simulation, you will consider whether fracking is an activity that should be managed by strict liability legal rules. You will read a news story revealing fracking harms that have occurred in your community, corporate background about the company engaging in fracking, a summary of what fracking is, Restatement excerpts, and procedural rule excerpts.

You have to consider whether you will take the plaintiff's case or not. In so considering, you will have to determine whether you have enough facts to plead a strict liability cause of action. Throughout this text, we have discussed the financial drivers of plaintiff's-side lawyering. In this simulation, you will consider these complexities directly as a lawyer. Will the costs of litigating the case exceed your recovery? Are the prospects for recovery too remote?

You will prepare for a client meeting with community activists, so there is a compelling human complexity to this case vetting too. If you cannot take the case, what reason will you cite? What role do lawyers play in their communities? Strict liability questions are heavily community-based and valued-laden. This simulation will also reveal how your own values may impact case selection. Is there more at stake in this case than just economic recovery?

———————

II. LOCAL NEWS STORY

FRACKING REAKS HAVOC ON SMALL TOWN OF LITTLE PLACE, TORTSYLVANIA

April 14, 9:09 a.m.

All was quiet in the town of Little Place until Big Oil & Drill Company showed up last year. In February, the fracking empire arrived and planted its drill less than half of a mile from the Apple Acres neighborhood.

It all began when Sally Smith noticed a change in the color of her faucet water. She called her plumber, thinking it was simply a problem with her pipes. Upon getting her water tested, it was found to be contaminated with arsenic and other toxins. Her plumber told her that she wasn't the only person he'd seen with these water toxins. He estimated fifteen to twenty homes he tested with the same exact issue, all on neighboring streets. Several members of the community have been left without drinking water, and forced to buy bottled water for their families.

But this isn't the only hardship this community is facing. It is hard to walk around town without hearing the coughing and the wheezing of both adults and children. Doctor Delores Day reports an increase of patients with moderate to severe asthma. The patients she's diagnosed have required treatment ranging from inhalers to breathing treatments multiple times a day. After speaking to Dr. Day directly, she stated that the patients she has diagnosed recently "have never showed symptoms or signs of asthma in the past." Dr. Day also reported an increase in her patients' blood pressure and several patients complaining of sleeping problems.

Other impacts of fracking are also raising concerns in the community. Javier Smith noticed cracks beginning to form in the walls of his home, and wallpaper peeling near the ceiling. Also, the local rabbit population has decreased significantly.

More than ten families have joined together seeking legal representation against the company due to problems that started just after the arrival of Big Oil. Big Oil has commented that their priority is the local community. A representative from Big Oil stated that the company utilizes methods of fracking with the lowest amounts of chemical additives. It has had no reported leaks or problems with the site at Little Place. They reject the notion that their company and drilling operation has caused these problems.

III. MEETING INQUIRY

TO: ATTORNEY

FROM: CONCERNED CITIZENS

DATE: APRIL 20

Dear Attorney,

We are a coalition of neighbors in Little Place, Tortsylvania. We got your name from the local Chamber of Commerce publication highlighting you as a rising star personal injury lawyer. You may have seen coverage of our plight in ABCD News last week. We are looking to hire a lawyer to represent us in a suit against Big Oil & Drill Company. Based on your website, we think your experience and expertise might be a good fit for our case.

Your website offered a free initial consultation. We would like to do an initial consult with you at your earliest convenience. Please advise of your willingness and interest in taking this potential case.

Candidly, two other firms have told us that they cannot take our case. We are quite disheartened trying to find representation. Thank you in advance for your time and guidance.

Sincerely,

Concerned Residents of Apple Acres

IV. FRACKING BACKGROUND RESEARCH

MEMORANDUM

From: Paralegal

To: Attorney

Re: Fracking Overview

Date: April 24

You asked me to summarize the fracking process for your prospective client meeting. Here are some preliminary notes for your review. Please let me know if you have any follow-up questions or research inquiries. Below is a useful image to depict the fracking process that I describe.

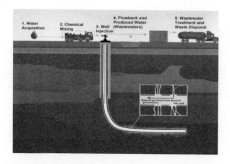

Figure 1: https://water.usgs.gov/owq/topics/hydraulic-fracturing/

Hydraulic fracturing, or fracking, is a drilling technique used to extract underground resources such as oil, natural gas, geothermal energy, and water. A well is constructed and then drilled hundreds or thousands of feet into the earth's surface. Lateral sections are then extended horizontally up to a mile from the vertical well, as depicted above.

Fracking fluid is then pumped into the well at a high pressure. The fracking fluid, while mostly water, also contains chemical additives. The pressure of the water fractures the rocks. Sand and ceramic particles are then pumped into the well to open the fractures further, releasing gas and oil. The pressure causes the fluids to flow back to the surface to be stored in disposal sites. These flowback fluids contain water and many contaminants, such as radioactive material, metals, hydrocarbons, and toxins. These fluids can also leak into the ground during the flowback process and cause pollution of the local water supply. I relied on Marc Lallanilla's *Facts About Fracking* article from Live Science dated February 10, 2018 in writing this memorandum (https://www.live science.com/34464-what-is-fracking.html).

Numerous studies document the health impacts of fracking, such as strokes, heart attacks, and asthma. I found several studies revealing increased high-risk pregnancies resulting in premature births, low birth rates, and infant deaths in affected pregnant women near drill and fracking sites.

These environmental and health effects are particularly acute in communities of color, low-income communities, rural communities, and indigenous communities. Your case strategy might be heavily informed by literature on environmental justice. Environmental justice seeks the fair treatment of communities on the basis of race, color, national origin, and income in developing and enforcing environmental laws, regulations, and policies. For litigation purposes, an environmental justice strategy would call into question how and why Big Oil was permitted to build these fracking wells in *our* community. These environmental disparities expose vulnerable communities, such as our own, unfairly to harms from fracking pollution.

A public records search revealed that Big Oil has nine wells and one wastewater disposal site in Little Place.

Our most recent United States Census data shows that 34% of Little Place's population is living in poverty. 17.4% of the community under the age of 65 are uninsured. Little Place's community is 16% Black or African American, 2% American Indian, 19% Hispanic or Latino, 4% Asian, 33% White, and 26% Two or More Races based on the most recent United States Census data.

V.   CORPORATE WEB SITE EXCERPT

Big Oil & Drill Company

About us

Big Oil & Drill Company was established in 1932 in Houston, Texas to find oil on American soil. Founder, Elan Jones, built the company on principles valuing community and family. Since then, Big Oil & Drill Company has worked to provide natural gas for the American people. It is our priority and mission to drill safely, create new jobs, and provide a more sustainable future in every community in which we enter.

To keep up with the energy revolution and reach the oil we need, we've begun using a process of hydraulic fracturing. We have worked to make it as safe as possible, using the farthest distance of any company between communities and our natural gas wells. We also have fewer additives in our drilling solution than any other company in the business.

Currently, we own and operate more drilling wells than any other company in America. We sell this oil to various businesses and industries to fuel America. We have brought in 1.2 billion dollars in revenue this year, and it keeps growing. We will not stop until America can sustain itself.

VI. LEGAL RESEARCH

(A) SUBSTANTIVE LAW

Legal research reveals that your state follows the strict liability rules outlined in the Restatement 2d of Torts §§ 519 and 520, which are excerpted below. The Restatement is not binding law. It is a highly authoritative secondary source summarizing the common law. Many courts, however, adopt specific sections as the binding state law. Tortsylvania has adopted these two provisions.

The Restatement 2d of Torts, § 519

(1) One who carries on an abnormally dangerous activity is subject to liability for harm to the person, land or chattels of another resulting from the activity, although he has exercised the utmost care to prevent the harm.

(2) This strict liability is limited to the kind of harm, the possibility of which makes the activity abnormally dangerous.

The Restatement 2d of Torts, § 520

In determining whether an activity is abnormally dangerous, the following factors are to be considered:

(a) existence of a high degree of risk of some harm to the person, land or chattels of others;

(b) likelihood that the harm that results from it will be great;

(c) inability to eliminate the risk by the exercise of reasonable care;

(d) extent to which the activity is not a matter of common usage;

(e) inappropriateness of the activity to the place where it is carried on; and

(f) extent to which its value to the community is outweighed by its dangerous attributes.

(B) PROCEDURAL RULES

Below are two short excerpts from the Federal Rules of Civil Procedure. Rule 8 advises you how to style a civil complaint for relief. This rule might inform your brainstorming of what claims are viable causes of action. Rule 12(b)(6) advises you how a defendant might try to dismiss a complaint for failure to state a claim. These are both federal rules that would apply in federal court. In civil procedure you will study whether a claim is brought in federal or state court. Many tort law cases will be state cases applying state rules of procedure. The federal rules are used for this simulation because it likely reinforces your civil procedure course content.

Rule 8. General Rules of Pleading

(a) Claim for Relief. A pleading that states a claim for relief must contain: * * *

(2) a short and plain statement of the claim showing that the pleader is entitled to relief; and

(3) a demand for the relief sought, which may include relief in the alternative or different types of relief.

Rule 12. How to Present Defenses

(b) Every defense to a claim for relief in any pleading must be asserted in the responsive pleading if one is required. But a party may assert the following defenses by motion:

* * *

(6) failure to state a claim upon which relief can be granted

VII. THE SIMULATION EXERCISE

In this simulation exercise, your firm will consider whether it can take a new case. You are meeting with the concerned citizens introduced in the preceding article and email. They need legal representation and they are struggling to find it. Your firm has scheduled a consultation, but it is not sure whether the case is viable yet.

You will apply the strict liability rules that you researched governing abnormally dangerous activities to the facts that you have about the case currently. You are convening as a law firm to prepare for the upcoming meeting with the prospective clients. Since you know the substance of the plaintiffs' concerns, you can prepare for the meeting by considering whether the facts—if true—support an argument strong enough to plead a complaint that will withstand a Motion to Dismiss.

You might take the facts and apply them to each factor of the Restatement test using the chart below. The residents' complaint would argue that fracking is an abnormally dangerous activity subject to strict liability. The plaintiffs want the chance to conduct discovery and learn more to prove their case.

The defendant will argue that there is insufficient evidence to support strict liability. The defendant will assert that ordinary negligence principles are enough and therefore the strict liability claim should be dismissed. Consider objectively the strength of your case and be prepared to discuss it at your law firm's meeting.

Restatement Factors	Arguments for Plaintiffs	Arguments for Defendant
(a) existence of a high degree of risk of some harm to the person, land or chattels of others		
(b) likelihood that the harm that results from it will be great		
(c) inability to eliminate the risk by the exercise of reasonable care		
(d) extent to which the activity is not a matter of common usage		
(e) inappropriateness of the activity to the place where it is carried on		
(f) extent to which its value to the community is outweighed by its dangerous attributes		

CHAPTER 12

DEFAMATION

I. INTRODUCTION

Defamation is a subject matter that bridges tort law and constitutional law. While bridging two substantial subject areas certainly makes the material more difficult to learn in an introductory torts class, popular news stories regularly cover defamation, providing helpful context and salience for students to master this material.

Defamation is an umbrella term that covers libelous (published) and slanderous (spoken) statements. Defamation allows a civil recovery for the harms caused by false statements. Defamation analysis examines what was said, whether it was false, and whether it harmed the plaintiff's reputation. For a statement to be untrue, it must be a fact, not an opinion.

Compensating the plaintiff for the defendant's harmful speech necessarily raises First Amendment constitutional questions regarding the defendant's right to utter the statements. This area of tort law accordingly raises interesting questions of competing societal values. How much latitude are we willing to give to speakers when their speech may cause harm to others? The answer depends, in part, on who is the subject of the speech. As a society, we are willing to give more latitude to speakers who utter false statements against public figures than statements against private figures. For defamatory statements against a public figure, malice is the level of proof required, while negligence is enough for private figures. Malice requires that the speaker knew the statement was false or acted with reckless disregard to the statement's truth. This is a higher standard because it reflects a societal value in favor of open public debate.

This analysis raises categorization issues for individuals who might be partially public for some purposes, but private generally. We clearly categorize politicians and movie stars as public figures. We easily categorize most of our neighbors, classmates, and coworkers as private figures generally. One can also become a public figure for a limited purpose only. For example, Chicago Cubs fans in my classes can instantly name Steve Bartman as the man who interfered with a foul ball in postseason play, even though the incident dates back to 2003! More recently, Christine Blasey Ford is also likely a limited-purpose public figure. Limited-purpose public figures will be held to the public figure standard only on the issue that brought them into public debate but will remain a private figure for all other purposes.

Proving reputational harm is a critical part of a defamation claim. The plaintiff has to bring forth witnesses and evidence suggesting that others have lowered their opinion of the plaintiff because of the defamatory statement. It can be difficult though to track and prove causality in a world of viral internet postings. The Internet has also vastly expanded the ability of defamatory statements to reach a wide audience rapidly. While this expands the reputational hit a plaintiff might take, the causation is hard to connect to any one speaker. Internet Service Providers are generally protected from liability for harms caused by posts on their sites and forums. For reputational harms, damages can be difficult to quantify. The plaintiff must prove loss of good standing in the community or the decreased respect and esteem of others.

This simulation exercise returns us back to the deaths that occurred at Sharp Shooter's Gun Range. We first learned about this case back in Chapter 1. As a reminder, a husband got a text from his wife telling him that she wanted a divorce. He fired his gun up in the air out of anger and frustration causing grave injuries.

This assignment reveals a negative review that was posted online speculating about the owner of the gun range personally. You will draft a demand letter to the author of the negative review seeking recovery for damages. You may also have drafted a demand letter in the Wrongful Death and Survival chapter, so this might be an opportunity to strengthen this skill further. Compare and contrast the relative strengths of the claims in Chapter 7 versus this Chapter. How does it alter your tone and posture?

———————

II. WEBSITE REVIEWS

Your research reveals the attached excerpts of Sharp Shooter's Gun Range's online reviews. The first batch precedes the shooting and the second follows it. The review that is prompting potential legal action is bracketed for your attention.

RateBiz.com Reviews

Sharp Shooter's Gun Range is locally-owned and operated by Chip Sharpe, a Palsgraf native. Established in 2004, Sharp Shooter's has the most comprehensive selection of firearms for rental or purchase and offers a variety of classes on safety and techniques.

Sharp Shooter's Gun Range

5339 Pistol Drive, Palsgraf, Tortsylvania 12345

4.6 ★★★★★   194 reviews   Sort by: Most relevant ▾   March 2

Tom Gunn
5 reviews

★★★★★ 3 weeks ago

This place is fantastic! I took my girlfriend here for our last date night and the employees were very helpful. She'd never been shooting before, so they went over everything with her until she felt comfortable with everything. We'll definitely be going back!

 Like

Annie Oak
1 review

★★★★★ 2 weeks ago

This is my favorite shooting range in the area. The prices are a little higher than other places, but it's worth it for the customer service and the quality of the facilities. I've taken some of their classes and my shooting has gotten way better, too!

 Like

Colt Fourtree
3 reviews

★★★★★ 2 months ago

I'm from Garretsburg and was just in Palsgraf for a few days visiting a friend. We went here and it was really cool. Top of the line facilities from what I can tell, and all of the employees are very friendly. Shout out to Ervin for getting us set up and for recommending a place to eat after!

 Like

RateBiz.com Reviews

Sharp Shooter's Gun Range is locally-owned and operated by Chip Sharpe, a Palsgraf native. Established in 2004, Sharp Shooter's has the most comprehensive selection of firearms for rental or purchase and offers a variety of classes on safety and techniques.

Sharp Shooter's Gun Range

5339 Pistol Drive, Palsgraf, Tortsylvania 12345

3.8 ★★★★☆   208 reviews   Sort by: Most relevant *   April 10

Karen
17 reviews
★☆☆☆☆   4 days ago

Worst range I've ever been to! Seriously, this must be a front for something, because otherwise it could NOT stay open as a gun range. Chip the owner is completely incompetent and has cut corners at every opportunity—he's obviously lining his pockets instead of running a safe business. I have never felt less safe while shooting a gun. No wonder someone DIED here recently!

 Like

> **Response from the owner** 4 days ago
> Hi Karen, I'm sorry this was your experience at Sharp Shooter's. We pride ourselves on having top-of-the-line safety features in our facility. I've run the business for 15 years now, and I can promise you I'm not lining my pockets with anything but lint. The range is my pet project and I do it because I love it. I looked at our guest logs from the last couple of weeks, and we didn't have any guest complaints during that time. Did you speak with an employee about feeling unsafe at any point? Our staff are trained to take guest safety seriously. And you're right that there was an incredibly unfortunate incident here lately, but it wasn't because we were cutting corners. We're doing everything we can to support those affected during this difficult time. I'd love to speak with you more about your experience. Please give us a call and I'd love to personally address your complaints.   -Chip Sharpe

Wes Smith
4 reviews

★★★★★ Yesterday

I've been coming here for years, and Sharp Shooter's is the real deal. The staff are knowledgeable and really nice, and the Owner, Chip, is a great guy. The place has gotten some bad press lately, but it doesn't deserve it. Give this place a "shot!"

 Like

Angie Lee
7 reviews

★★☆☆☆ 1 week ago

I heard someone got shot here recently? My friends and I won't be going back until they fix whatever is wrong. Sad, it always seemed like a cool place and I never had a problem there, but you can't be too careful these days...

 Like

III. CORRESPONDENCE

Palsgraf SafeStreets Project
"Keeping our community safe from gun violence."

June 19

Palsgraf SafeStreets Project
1100 Main Street, Palsgraf, TS 12345
(293) 994-1732
palsgraf@safestreets.com
www.palsgrafsafestreets.org

Chip Sharpe
Owner
Sharp Shooter's Gun Range
5339 Pistol Drive, Palsgraf, TS 12345

Mr. Sharpe:

We want to thank you for all that you have done in your time as a Board Member of the Palsgraf SafeStreets Project. Your knowledge and expertise have been invaluable over the last five years.

Unfortunately, in light of recent events at your company, we must respectfully ask you to resign from your position on PSSP's Board of Directors. You may recall that our bylaws clearly state that any Board Member who is involved in a gun-related crime or lawsuit will no longer be permitted to serve on our Board. As Palsgraf's leading nonprofit organization devoted to reducing gun violence in our community, I'm sure you understand why we cannot have Board Members associated with deadly incidents involving firearms. The legislative session is just about to begin again with critical gun safety resolutions pending. We hope you understand that our cause—making our communities safer—is bigger than any one leader or board member. Lives are on the line. We need to prioritize the mission and the integrity of our organization above all else. While we hoped that the public scrutiny you faced would blow over, we need to move forward with our mission.

We have prorated your board stipend. We will be issuing a check for $3,000. We will not be paying the remaining stipend of $4,000.

Again, we thank you for your contributions to the organization over the years. We hope that you will continue to support our cause in the future.

We wish you all the best as you work to rebuild your business and your reputation.

Sincerely,

Sue Safeton
Chairman, Board of Directors
Palsgraf SafeStreets Project

IV. LEGAL RESEARCH

Your legal research identified the following elements to prove defamation in Tortsylvania.

A plaintiff must prove the following for a defamation suit involving a private figure:

(1) a statement of fact;

(2) that is false;

(3) and defamatory;

(4) of and concerning the plaintiff;

(5) that is published to a third party;

(6) not absolutely or conditionally privileged;

(7) that causes actual injury;

(8) that is the result of fault by the defendant;

(9) that causes special (pecuniary) harm in addition to generalized reputational injury.

V. THE SIMULATION EXERCISE

We learn in the preceding materials that Chip Sharpe is facing scrutiny for the recent events at his business premises. He has come to your law firm for help. He is devastated by the loss of life that occurred on this property. He urgently needs to restore his business livelihood though.

He is very frustrated by the negative commentary online. He is particularly distraught over the business reviews attacking him personally. This review from Karen Meene particularly haunts your client. He has already reached out to the Internet Service Provider to have the review removed. RateBiz.com told Chip that it would only remove the review with a court order. It also informed Chip that the original poster can review the post at her election.

Use the legal rule provided in your materials to write a demand letter for Chip Sharpe's individual defamation claim against Karen Meene, the author of the negative online review. A demand letter is an incredibly useful tool in lawyering. The goal in writing a demand letter is to try to convince the other party to settle the case as opposed to litigating it. Taking a case to trial is costly and time consuming for all parties involved. By laying out your client's case against the other party and specifying the damages you are seeking, you are giving the other party a chance to end the conflict at the outset.

To write a demand letter, begin with a concise version of the facts. Be specific regarding when certain events occurred and in demonstrating how the other party is at fault. This likely includes stating the elements of defamation and clarifying how Karen Meene is liable for her statements. Finally, state the damages that your client is seeking. Include documentation for the quantifiable damages, and evidence to support the intangible damages, such as reputational harm. Give the other party a deadline by which to respond. Close by letting the other party know that if you do not receive the amount or action requested, you will file a lawsuit. Always remember to be professional and polite.

Think carefully here about your client's objectives. What are you actually demanding in this letter? What persuasive tools are most likely to benefit your client? What amount of damages, if any, are you seeking? What if your claim is very weak or potentially non-viable? How will that alter your tone and rhetoric?